THE COMPLETE CHRISTIAN

THE COMPLETE CHRISTIAN
A Guide to Living

Alex Basile

ST PAULS

Library of Congress Cataloging-in-Publication Data

Basile, Alex.
  The complete Christian : a guide to living / by Alex Basile.
    p. cm.
  ISBN-13 978-0-8189-1325-9
  ISBN-10: 0-8189-1325-8
  1. Christian life—Catholic authors. I. Title.
  BX2350.3.B378 2010
  248.4'82—dc22
                                    2010008969

Produced and designed in the United States of America by the
Fathers and Brothers of the Society of St. Paul,
2187 Victory Boulevard, Staten Island, New York 10314-6603
as part of their communications apostolate.

ISBN 10: 0-8189-1325-8
ISBN -13: 978-0-8189-1325-9

Printing Information:

Current Printing - first digit	1	2	3	4	5	6	7	8	9	10

Year of Current Printing - first year shown

2010	2011	2012	2013	2014	2015	2016	2017	2018	2019

ACKNOWLEDGMENTS

To Allison, Alex and Maggie
for your daily inspiration and giving me the gift of your love.

To Christine Phillips
for your help in editing and formatting this book.

To Jeff Harris and Justin Michelena
for lending your talents in photography and graphic design.

To Father Thomas Cardone
who guides me through every project with
your friendship and mentoring.

I dedicate this book to my parents,
Al and Eileen Basile
who have shown me the possibility
of being a complete Christian each and every day.

TABLE OF CONTENTS

Part Five:
SCULPTING THE SOUL

Part Six:
FINDING GOLD IN YOUR RELATIONSHIPS

PREFACE

Once again Alex Basile invites us to take a further step in our journey towards fulfilling our Baptismal Vocation. What does it mean to be fully immersed in the Christian life? What does it mean to be Christian or to have "Christ-in" me? Is Christ truly within me?

Am I a complete Christian? We often live our Christianity in name. Yes, I am a Roman Catholic. Yes, I am an Evangelical Christian. Yes, I believe in Jesus as Lord and Savior. However, do the people who surround my daily life, see Christ operating in me? This is a good question to ponder.

If I am a true Christian, people can recognize this by what I say and what I do. When I live the gospel life, my Christianity will be contagious. Or as Blessed William Joseph Chaminade says, when we are Christians, we are all missionaries of Jesus through the intercession of Mary.

Alex introduces us to a change of heart and mind that will eventually prompt us to be stronger missionaries who desire to turn ourselves over completely to Christ. He then suggests venues for this missionary action. For as St. James says: "What good is there to have faith without practicing it?"

I believe that the reader will be consumed by Alex's contemporary examples as he paves the way to a complete Christian lifestyle. Where does he begin? Father Chaminade, one of Alex's spiritual mentors always taught that "the essential is the interior." Alex learned this at an early age in high school and has been convinced that any Christian must develop an inner life that is rooted in the person of Jesus. This inner life then becomes a springboard to becoming missionary. Only when this is accomplished can an individual continue to move forward in faith.

As you allow this spirit of *The Complete Christian* to take root in the mind and heart, obstacles to holiness will become more manageable, the essentials of faith will become clearer and the importance of self-knowledge and the value of relationships will become paramount in the Christian journey.

May the Father and the Son and the Holy Spirit be glorified in all places through the Immaculate Virgin Mary!

Father Thomas A. Cardone, S.M.
Chaplain, Kellenberg Memorial

THE GREATEST GIFT

Recently, a colleague of mine gave me a copy of the movie called *The Ultimate Gift*. She used the film on a retreat and spoke about how the students loved its message. The movie centers on the last will and testament of billionaire Red Stevens. As the will is read by his lawyer, each relative is told why they are not receiving the money they expected. After each relative has heard their final message from Red, they must exit the boardroom. This leaves Jason, the grandson of Red, as the only remaining relative who has not yet heard what he will receive from the will. In order for Jason to receive his "gift" from his grandfather, he must complete certain tasks. Each job that Jason completes will bring him closer to his inheritance. The goal of his grandfather was to cure the spiritual blindness of his grandson that had kept him from seeing some of life's greatest gifts. By the end of the story Jason learns the value of friendship, work, family, education and love. I won't spoil the end of the movie but I will tell you that the conversion of Jason is a pivotal part of the movie. He transforms from a greedy and selfish person, to become a man who understands the importance of love and relationships.

> A life incorporating Jesus Christ allows us to complete the tasks that unlock the gifts of love, friendship, work and family.

We too are beneficiaries of the "will of the Father." Our tasks involve both repentance and renewal which enable us to embrace the conversion that we all need in anticipation of our greatest gift, Jesus Christ. Born in a stable, He began a humble existence on Earth. He spent His days in Nazareth where He grew in knowledge and wisdom. Jesus established His Church through His disciples. He was betrayed and sacrificed on a Cross for the sins of humanity. The gift of His sacrifice freed us from the chains that kept us from entering union with God. A life incorporating Jesus Christ allows us to complete the tasks that unlock the gifts of love, friendship, work and family. Baptism begins our journey with Christ that hopefully ends in heaven. Our infinite happiness depends upon whether or not we embrace His presence.

We tend to compartmentalize our lives. We separate the spiritual from the mundane. Prayer life becomes disjointed from everyday living. Our challenge is to keep Christ alive morning, noon and night. No one can be a part-time Christian. We lock Jesus away in church and once the door closes, we leave Him behind.

The purpose of *The Complete Christian* is to initiate the reflective process of how to incorporate Jesus into our everyday lives. We must learn to unlock the tabernacle and unveil His presence into every aspect of our being. We should not save God for Sunday alone. An existence filled with Jesus gives everything deeper meaning. He shows us that everything is of consequence.

Every action and every relationship has bearing on this life and the next. Jesus desires to walk beside us. Allow Him to work within your life. Let Him touch your relationships. He will make your joys greater and He will lessen your sorrows. Jesus will carry you when you think your burdens are too great.

The following chapters deal with the avenues of life that affect every Christian. Ask yourself where Jesus fits into these aspects of living. Bring Christ with you on your great adventure. Each chapter of your life should include Him. Put on Christ and show Him to the world. Recognize Jesus along your journey. He lives deep within each person you encounter. While on earth, Jesus performed miracles and rose from the dead. He made it clear to those He encountered who He was. Yet, they still rejected Him. We insist Jesus is part of our lives, but we nonchalantly put Him at the bottom of our priorities. Accept the gift He gives to you and all humanity. Don't take it for granted. Open this gift and share it with those around you.

PART ONE
LOOKING INWARD

RAISING THE BAR

"The Christian life is not a constant high. I have my moments
of deep discouragement. I have to go to God in prayer with tears
in my eyes, and say, 'O God, forgive me,' or 'Help me.'"
Billy Graham

In my second year at Kellenberg Memorial High School, I had
the responsibility of escorting the Junior candidates to their Eucharistic Minister training day. During one of the presentations,
Father Jerry told the students about their moral responsibilities
in their new ministry. He explained to them that people would
look to them for spiritual leadership. Others would notice how
they acted on Friday night at a party or how they treated others
in the hallway at school. He said, "A person should not hold
the Body of Christ on Sunday and tear someone apart with
their words on Monday." As I pondered those words, I won-
dered how his statement applied to me. I realized that Father
Jerry's words dealt with more than just those who distributed
the Body of Christ, they called all of us who are part of His
Body to act a certain way. Christ walked in our shoes to give
us a clear example of how to live. Jesus didn't simply lecture
and post a list of "do's" and "don'ts." Jesus acted as He wanted
us to act; He loved as He wanted us to love and forgave as He
wanted us to forgive. Christians must immerse themselves into

the attitude of Jesus. We call ourselves His followers, but many times we forget why we bear His name. Ask yourself, "Do I act a particular way because I am a Christian?" and "Am I mindful of Jesus as I make decisions?" Evolving as a Christian means striving to become more like Jesus.

A life in Christ can lead us to heavenly treasure. This great hope should bring us great joy; however, we allow the worries of this world to drag us down. We become consumed with mundane concerns and lose our focus on His Kingdom. The Christian must be the light in a world of darkness. We must be the eyes of the blind and a hand to the lost. When people look at us, they should see the inner joy that Christ brings. In our sorrows, we are united with Him on Good Friday and in our triumphs we rise with Him on Easter Sunday.

We do not need to set up shop on the local corner to become His messengers. Our witness to the Gospels should make us His best representatives. Our consolation and peace should be apparent to those we meet. The way we greet the stranger on the line at the supermarket or the way we act in traffic, should make Jesus a reality to others. We must be the living billboards to Christ. In a world that rains its misery on its citizens, we can provide shelter from the storm. There are so many people, including Christians, who forget about the secret to true happiness. We spend our lives searching for something that we already possess. Jesus dwells within every one of us, waiting to recognize Him. We start to resemble some of the first disciples who failed to realize that it was Jesus who was with them on the road to Emmaus:

> Then they returned from the tomb and announced all
> these things to the eleven and to all the others. The

women were Mary Magdalene, Joanna, and Mary the mother of James; the others who accompanied them also told this to the Apostles, but their story seemed like nonsense and they did not believe them. But Peter got up and ran to the tomb, bent down, and saw the burial cloths alone; then he went home amazed at what had happened. Now that very day two of them were going to a village seven miles from Jerusalem called Emmaus, and they were conversing about all the things that had occurred. And it happened that while they were conversing and debating, Jesus Himself drew near and walked with them, but their eyes were prevented from recognizing Him. He asked them, "What are you discussing as you walk along?" They stopped, looking downcast. One of them, named Cleopas, said to Him in reply, "Are you the only visitor to Jerusalem who does not know of the things that have taken place there in these days?" And He replied to them, "What sort of things?" They said to Him, "The things that happened to Jesus the Nazarene, who was a prophet mighty in deed and word before God and all the people, how our chief priests and rulers both handed Him over to a sentence of death and crucified Him. But we were hoping that He would be the one to redeem Israel; and besides all this, it is now the third day since this took place. Some women from our group, however, have astounded us: they were at the tomb early in the morning and did not find His body; they came back and reported that they had indeed seen a vision of angels who announced that He was alive. Then some of those with us went to the tomb and found things just as the women had described, but Him they did not see." And He said to them, "Oh, how foolish you are! How slow of heart to believe all that the prophets spoke!" (Luke 24:9-25)

We must ask the question, "Why were these disciples leaving Jerusalem?" If they had heard the incredible news of the Resurrection, wouldn't they want to remain in the city? Why walk to Emmaus when everything is erupting with amazement in Jerusalem? Do we also walk in the wrong direction? We consider ourselves His disciples, but we too struggle to see Him even though He makes His presence known to us. We become distracted by trivial matters and forget our true purpose. We bind ourselves to Jesus in name only. We neglect to put our faith into action.

I often use this analogy with my students: How would you react if someone who considered themselves a huge Yankee fan answered these questions in the following way?

"Who is your favorite current player?"
They responded, "Mickey Mantle. "When was the last time you watched a Yankee game on television or at the stadium?" They answered, "I never watch the games, and I am way too busy!"

We would be perplexed by these answers. For someone to be considered a true fan, they seem out of touch. I ask my students, "If we call ourselves Christians and we do not follow Jesus as we should, are we truly His disciples?" Are *we* walking away from Him, when we ought to be seeking His glory? Most of my students agree that we would have failed in our obligations to Him. I often contemplate whether or not I measure up to the standards that Jesus puts before me. When others see me at a bar, in my car, or in the faculty room, do they see me as an example of Jesus or just another guy?

> If we call ourselves Christians and we do not follow Jesus as we should, are we truly His disciples?

How do you measure up to His standards? Do your friends, family and colleagues see you as someone they would like to emulate? Ask yourself the following:

"Am I raising the bar to Christ or am I just coasting through life?" "Am I driving others crazy or am I leading them to compassionate lives?" "Am I building community with my fellow collaborators in Jesus or am I a splintering element of negativity in the Body of Christ?"

As a teacher of the faith, I spend every day speaking to people of the importance of a Christocentric life. Most students listen intently, but only a few make a point to live it. We talk about Jesus and how much we admire Him. We are hesitant to make the radical changes that He demands. Following Christ cannot be like choosing items off of an a la carte menu. To be a complete Christian, we must accept the whole package. Jesus challenges His disciples to live up to tough standards. Step up to meet Him. We must tear down the walls that separate us from God. Each day without Him deprives us from rising to our potential. Prove yourself worthy of being called a disciple. Turn around and go back to Him.

A CHANGE OF HEART

"God is not glorified in any transaction upon earth
so much as in the conversion of a sinner."

Archibald Alexander

Over the past ten years, the books of Mitch Albom have sat atop *The New York Times* bestseller list. The book that launched Albom into superstardom was his classic *Tuesdays with Morrie*. In 1997, *Tuesdays* received a tremendous boost when Oprah Winfrey endorsed his book. The book chronicled the reunion of a teacher, Morrie Schwartz, with his student, Mitch Albom, sixteen years after their separation. Once Mitch had graduated from Brandeis University, he lost contact with his favorite teacher. Morrie is dying from Lou Gehrig's disease. Always a teacher, Morrie desired to leave Mitch with one final lesson. Many people have been touched by Morrie's existential advice.

One of the central themes of the book deals with Morrie's spiritual journey throughout his life. Morrie grew up in a Jewish family. After Morrie's mother died at age eight, Morrie abandoned his faith life. Morrie spent most of his adult life as an agnostic. The suffering in his life had caused Morrie to give up on his relationship with God. After being diagnosed with ALS, Morrie contemplated his mortality. He underwent a spiritual conversion. He began speaking to God through prayer. He asked God if He would consider making Morrie one of His "angels." Impending death can certainly change our spiritual priorities. Churches are filled with people "cramming for finals." Some neglect God the majority of life only to recognize the importance of a heavenly relationship in their later years. Why wait until then? Jesus called everyone to change their lives. When He told His followers, "The Kingdom of God is at hand," He wanted us to sense the urgency to embrace God now! He wanted us to look inwardly and discover how we can become better people. We can bring about change in our lives through conversion. We not only change the way we act, we change the way we think. Jesus wants us to alter the course of our lives. Selfishness drives us away from God, while repentance turns our hearts back to Him.

Properly focusing on God requires a change of consciousness. Jesus constantly prompts us to reevaluate our lives. Whether we attend Mass daily or never pray, we all need to examine where we stand in our relationship with God. Since sin flaws humanity, we desperately need spiritual healing. The Church gives us special times throughout the year to focus on conversion; however, we should not wait for the liturgical seasons of Advent and Lent to change our hearts. Conversion must become an ongoing process.

> True conversion requires us to stop worrying about
> what others think.

Recognize your faults and deal with them. Sometimes we need to "remove the plank" from our eye to see the truth about ourselves. Too many people play the denial game. Spiritual blindness is a common ailment of humanity today. If you are not able to recognize the obstacles that keep you from having a truer relationship with God and others, ask those who know you the best about the faults that you need to address.

Our priorities determine our actions. We must ask the question, "Do I forsake others when something better comes along?" I know I have. Make sure that people know where they fit into your life. When things go wrong, ask others to forgive you. Forgiveness is a major part of the conversion process. We must admit our faults to others. We must make a solemn promise to rectify the problem and then ask how we can make the situation better.

Think constantly about new ways to reinvent yourself. When I first came to teach, I couldn't believe the amount of vacation time given to us. I had formerly been in my own business where I opened on every holiday including Christmas. I quickly realized that I needed these vacations to rejuvenate myself, especially summer vacation. I took my summers to contemplate the areas that I wanted to grow over the next year. I enter each year with a "to do" list. This process has proved successful in my personal and professional growth. Step back and make your own personal list of improvements that you would like to make in your life. Give yourself a "spiritual make-over." Evaluate your priorities and see where God and others rate. Consider what you and your life look like to others. Surround yourself with things that will spark your faith life. The latest tabloid or your favorite sitcom might provide some light entertainment; however incorporate some spiritually enlightening material as well.

> One of Jesus' greatest lessons shows us that
> conformity can make us miserable.

Bookstores hold a vast treasure of books that can elevate your soul, and amazingly there are shows that deal with real Christian issues. Once you have immersed yourself into a world of faith, you will start to notice a tremendous difference.

True conversion requires us to stop worrying about what others think. Looking at the life of Jesus makes us realize that He didn't go along with the crowd. One of His greatest lessons shows us that conformity can make us miserable. The rich young man walks away from Jesus because he is unwilling to accept the radical challenge of the Teacher. The young man lived a decent, moral existence, but was unwilling to take the next step in his spiritual conversion. He shows us that conforming to the ways of the material world makes it difficult for us to separate. The path to God is overgrown with obstacles. The saying, "What is popular is not always right, and what is right is not always popular" enforces this point. Seek your own road. Others may not lead, but they will follow. People admire pioneers who pave the way. Be a moral trendsetter. You may inspire others to change as well.

Learn to live like today is your last day. Like Morrie, death can help us to look at the way we live. It puts things in perspective. Death makes everything else sweeter. Live each day as if it were a precious gift. Every conversation will have meaning and understanding. Procrastination will dissipate. Prayer will take on greater importance.

The story of Saint Augustine remains one of the most memorable conversion stories in Christianity. Augustine lived a morally loose life. He resided with a young woman and had a son out of wedlock. Augustine followed certain philosophers only to become disillusioned. After listening to Saint Ambrose speak in Milan, Augustine gained an appreciation for the Scriptures and Christian life. Saint Augustine's famous prayer said:

> You have made us for Yourself Lord, and our hearts are restless until they rest in You.

Augustine knew the chaos in a life without God. Saint Ambrose and the Scriptures brought Saint Augustine to the truth of Jesus as the Word. Conversion means living according to the Word. Allow your connection with Jesus to change you for the better. Don't wait; the time to change is now! Repent!

THE MAN IN THE MIRROR

3

"The greatest success is successful self-acceptance."

Ben Sweet

When I owned my delicatessen, the amount of hours I worked each week made it difficult to complete my errands. During this period, one of our cooks volunteered to cut my hair. Pat had been trained as a beautician and practiced her craft at her house. There were many weeks that I had to work more than eighty hours. Since I didn't have the time to leave the store, Pat said that she would cut my hair after her shift ended in our kitchen. The beautician and the barber hold similar responsibilities as bartenders and psychologists. They listen to people tell their stories as they complete their task. Pat and I usually engaged in pleasantries about the deli and life. But one day I started a discussion about one of man's biggest fears, hair loss. In our discussion, I rationalized that I would never lose my hair because my two grandfathers had a substantial amount until they passed away. My father's dad had hair like Brillo. His barber often complained about the density of his "mane" as he attempted to get his scissors through it. "I could never lose my hair with genes like that"! I boasted to Pat. Suddenly, there was an awkward silence. I quickly lost my confidence. "What do *you* think, Pat?" I begged. Pat gingerly revealed the truth that only my barber would know; I had started to lose my hair. I clung to the day when I considered myself the fifth Beatle, at least follically. Pat responded as a doctor does when answering the difficult questions of a patient in distress. "Well I think your hair is thinning a little" she said honestly. "This couldn't be!" I thought as I sat there helplessly.

My grandfathers never had to deal with this problem, but my father did. God gives and God takes away. I quickly came to the realization that some things are out of our control. The pharmacist who worked down the block wanted me to try Rogaine. The effects of the new drug made me dizzy. I quickly gave up on that experiment. The abandonment of that drug accelerated my "hair problems." Surprisingly, my hair (or lack of it) never bothered me. I have had endless discussions about my dilemma. "Doesn't it bother you?" many people have asked. About thirty percent of men experience hair loss. In my office at school, I have a picture of my wife Allison and me before we married. When people see my before and after pictures, they favor the way I look now. "The way you look now becomes you," they assure me. I appreciate their compliments, but every day I have to account to only one person, the man in the mirror. We must love ourselves for who we are. We stand at the altar of self-acceptance every day. The ritual begins when we approach the mirror in our bathroom every morning. We look at ourselves and think about what we want to change about ourselves, rather than what we love about ourselves. As a teacher, I deal with self-esteem issues every day. Many of my students fail to recognize their external or inner beauty. They overlook their true talents. "I have nothing to offer," they exclaim in frustration. Our culture fuels the fire of self-doubt. The ads echo in our restless minds: we need to be thin, we need to have a full head of hair, we need to be rich, and we must be successful. Society holds us to extreme standards that seem difficult to reach. These goals never include happiness and self-acceptance. Looking in the mirror each day can be a difficult task. We scrutinize our faults more than anyone. We become our harshest critics. There are things we must consider in our quest for self-acceptance.

Discover your talents. Find your passion in life. Once you complete the tasks that are expected of you, explore your loves. No matter what you think or feel, everyone has their own unique talent and ability that they bring to the world. Sometimes these abilities evolve organically, and sometimes need to be cultivated by the prompting of others. We never know if we can succeed at anything until we try. The greatest musicians and athletes dedicate tireless hours to their passions. Nothing comes without a price.

Stop being too critical about your faults. Be gentle on yourself. When we look in the mirror, we tend to focus on the things that bother us. This human tendency can make anyone dwell on the negative. Focus on the positive. Examine the things that you do best and discover how to bring your gifts to others. Our talents were never meant to remain hidden. Stop keeping your secret from the world. Yearly, I learn of a student who escaped my grasp by staying out of the spotlight and never revealing their talent to me or our school community. "I would have put you on our CD's," I protest. They seem unfazed by my plea. "People would know that I sing," they respond defensively. "Exactly!" I respond. Their talent would be recognized by three thousand people instantly. From Uniondale to the Solomon Islands, many would be touched by their own translation of the Gospel. They never understand the magnitude of their decision. Show the world your best. Bear the criticism and grow in your talent.

> The more we love others, the more we can love ourselves.

The generosity that we extend to others makes us think differently about ourselves. Practice simple acts of kindness every day. The more we emulate Jesus in our lives, the more we find true happiness. We must overcome selfishness. Selfishness robs us from loving ourselves and others as we are supposed to. The more we love others, the more we can love ourselves. The process of giving yourself to others will change the way you see yourself in the mirror.

When things go wrong, laugh at yourself. Life is too short to take ourselves too seriously. Laughter lifts the weariest of souls. G.K. Chesterton said, "Angels fly because they take themselves lightly." A sense of humor can help us through any situation. Laughter can deflect feelings of anger, guilt and stress. The more we laugh at ourselves, the more we can accept our flaws and imperfections. One of the most interesting characteristics of the Gospels is that they never describe what Jesus looks like. There was only one person who had to be satisfied with His appearance and that was Himself. Every day should be a person's quest for self-satisfaction. We must look in the mirror and accept who we are. This step is necessary for us to "love others as ourselves," as Jesus commanded. Self-love is the seed that blossoms into the garden of our love for humanity. Love yourself and appreciate the uniqueness that you bring to the world. Practice the love of Jesus, but do not exclude yourself. He loves you, so love yourself as well.

Becoming A Complete Christian
Part One – Looking Inward

Read Luke 19:1-10 and reflect on the following questions:

1. What are the ways that I show or do not show the world that I am a Christian?

2. How can I bring more of Jesus' influence into my life?

3. How am I at times like Zacchaeus?

4. When people look at me, what do they see?

5. What are my greatest attributes and how can I share them with others?

6. What do I dislike about myself? How can I change these things?

PART TWO
CREATING THE RIGHT ATMOSPHERE

COUNTERING 4 THE CULTURE

"The culture we have does not make people feel good
about themselves. And you have to be strong enough to say if
the culture doesn't work, don't buy it."

Morrie Schwartz

Each year I show my senior religion class a few clips from the
movie, *Going My Way*. I want to give them a glimpse of the ideal
Church and the beauty of a simpler time. Their initial groans as
the black and white movie begins turn to pleas to watch more
of the movie. *Going My Way* was released in 1944. It won seven
Academy Awards, including best picture. A younger priest,
Father O'Malley played by Bing Crosby, is sent to reform a
parish that has declined under the care of its older pastor (Barry
Fitzgerald). The film received tremendous critical and public
acclaim. Its sequel, *The Bells of St. Mary's* also became a classic.
My students notice the stark differences between this movie
and the shows of today. I use this as an opportunity to discuss
the appetite of our culture for superficial programming. We
discuss how television has evolved from the days of its earliest
programs.

In the 1950's, in the midst of *I Love Lucy, The Milton Berle
Show, The Honeymooners* and *The Frank Sinatra Show,* a unique

show drew huge viewers each week. *Life Is Worth Living*, a show that featured the sermons of Archbishop Fulton Sheen, a New York cleric and author, captured a large portion of the viewing audience. At its peak, Sheen had more than thirty million people tune in to see his show. People from every faith and background wanted to hear his pearls of wisdom about life and living. Sheen magnetized America with his piercing eyes and practical advice. Many recognized him as a modern prophet. His show became stiff competition against some of the most popular shows of all time.

When you take the television and movie line-up of the 1950's and 1960's and compare it to today, you see stark differences. In the show *I Love Lucy*, the censors struggled with how to deal with Lucy's pregnancy. They banned the use of the word "pregnant." They also required Lucy and Ricky to sleep in separate beds. When the parents in *The Brady Bunch* were seen in bed kissing "good night" the censors were furious. Today, we bear a barrage of sexual innuendoes and, worse yet, blatant sexual acts on a nightly basis. There is very little left to the imagination.

> We must use what Jesus gave us to counter the effects of this culture.

Today, there also seems to be a real resistance to the God-centered and spiritual when it comes to the media world. When the movie, *The Passion of the Christ* previewed, people protested calling the film "too gory" and "anti-Semitic." In an age when we delight in watching people squirm on reality shows, would people embrace Bishop Sheen's program? In a society where we have pushed God out of our public schools, would our young people see Bishop Sheen as some kind of alien? As Christians, we understand our need for nourishment. Jesus provides our daily bread which sustains us and transforms us. But what happens when we become immersed in the "culture of death"? We must use what Jesus gave us to counter the effects of this culture. These are some simple ways to protect ourselves and others:

Filter out the negative aspects of the media. Turn off the garbage. It is way too easy to watch a program that degrades us rather than elevates who we are. Pay attention to language and the way people speak to each other in the shows that you watch. The media portrays the dysfunctional family as the norm. We all have some level of dysfunction in our families, but our hope is that we can repair our difficulties and rise above our problems. We can certainly withstand more reality than the idealistic *Brady Bunch* or *Father Knows Best*, but we can aim higher than the vulgarity of *South Park*.

The culture teaches that sex is merely for pleasure. It becomes a quest or even a contest to see who can engage in sexual activity first or most often. The *American Pie* movies trivialized sexuality. The group of young adults challenged each other to lose their virginity. Suddenly, a sacred act became a disposable act of pleasure. Realize that the media's version of the ideal body is part of the fantasy world of Hollywood. Computer graphics transform the normal characteristics of the imperfect body into the unattainable. Those who strive for "perfection" often fall into the world of eating disorders. Live healthy and within the limits of what God has given you. Don't deprive your body simply to fit into the Hollywood image.

> Don't buy into the consumerism philosophy of "the more we have, the happier we will be."

Look at your life and evaluate what you need to live well. Trim the fat. Ask yourself if you need to buy the newest version of a product that you already own. Do we upgrade our possessions simply out of habit? Are we trying to keep up with the "Joneses"? When the urge rises to buy the latest and the best, allow some time to pass. If you still feel the need to have the object, you may truly need it. Many times, our impulses lead us astray. The material world can leave us feeling empty and unfulfilled. Don't buy into the consumerism philosophy of "the more we have, the happier we will be."

Put a new perspective on politics. The political world has been divided into the categories of Republicans and Democrats, Conservatives and Liberals. We fight battles that only one side can win. Work for justice and truth in society. Help end the waste in government and utilize resources to help everyone. There are too many people starving and homeless in the shadows of where we live and work. Fight for the sanctity of life and bring the cause of the unborn and the aging to the consciousness of those around you.

Make it your mission to place God back in society. Some people fear a theocracy and preach the separation of Church and State. The presence of God has been all but erased from the media. Even Christ has been removed from Christmas. Don't permit the small percentage of those who refuse to believe to remove God from our midst. We sing "God Bless America" and say "One nation under God," because we understand that our great nation was founded by people who wanted the freedom to worship. Keep God present in society. Heroes died so you could have the right. Jesus died to give you even more. Make your sacrifice.

A few years ago Kellenberg Memorial High School cancelled its Senior Prom. The administration of Kellenberg saw that the prom had clearly become an event that was not conducive to the school philosophy. There was a tremendous amount of coverage from the press around the country. People couldn't seem to fathom that a school would actually forego such a big event. The school took a stand against the sexual activity and underage drinking associated with the prom. As a chaperone at the prom, I witnessed a few years where the crowd had dwindled to less than half after only a few hours. In what had been an exodus for Manhattan that began at 11 p.m., it had now shifted to 9 p.m. departure for the Hamptons. In a letter to a parent, Father Philip Eichner, the school president and Brother Kenneth Hoagland, the school's principal, stated that the prom had become an "over-projected and expensive formal show." They reminded the parents that in the Christian community this is called "vanity," emptiness. The administration came up with an alternative cruise around New York City. It is a non-formal, exclusive school event that brings the senior class together for one last time before graduation. Most students seem to prefer this event, especially since it has eliminated the pressure to find a date for the evening.

The Kellenberg prom event was a courageous stand against the culture. Our culture can be extremely blind and dangerous. Our responsibilities as Christians include bringing sanity to a world in chaos. As Jesus calmed the turbulent sea, He also calmed the hearts of those He encountered. We must bring His peace to our world. Jesus came into this world to create a new culture; promote His culture of peace and love in everything you do.

MOTHERLY  ADVICE

"Whoever does not wish to have Mary Immaculate as his Mother
will not have Christ as his Brother..."

St. Maximilian Kolbe

The historians of Jesus' time rarely, if ever, mention the little town of Nazareth. Probably less than a hundred people inhabited the tiny village. Mary and Joseph were typical parents. They loved their child and wanted the best for Him. They taught Him the ways of a person growing up in Nazareth. This was the place where He would grow "in age and wisdom." He followed the rules of a devout Jewish home. If you walked through the narrow streets, you would probably have heard Mary calling out the window reminding her son to assist His father in the carpenter's shop, rather than goofing off with His buddies. As His mother, she made Jesus aware of His responsibilities around the house. The candid exchange at Cana showed us that Mary did not hesitate to speak her mind. Like all families, they experienced both good and bad times. The Holy Family gave us an example of how to live in humility and simplicity.

> Mary shows us the true meaning of "discipleship."

From the time of Jesus, people noticed Mary as a leader. She earned the title as Queen of the Apostles through her quiet but strong presence. Mary takes her place in Christianity as the Mother of All. As the person closest to Jesus, we can learn a tremendous amount from Mary.

Mary shows us the meaning of true discipleship. When she responds with her Fiat, we learn that Mary understands the importance of handing herself over completely to God. Today, our response to the angel Gabriel probably would be, "What's in it for me?" Mary surrendered her life to the will of God. The reward for her faith was a life "full of grace." God calls Mary into service and she responds without hesitation, "Let it be done to me according to your word." Discipleship can put us face to face with the unthinkable. At the foot of the Cross, Mary's fiat takes on a whole new meaning. Mary silently and faithfully hands her Son over to be sacrificed for humanity. She showed us that we must embrace the Paschal Mystery as she did. Speak your own fiat and respond to God's call like Mary. Follow her Son on the road to the Cross. You may encounter sorrow along the way, but in the end His glory awaits you.

> Mary tells us the secret to life:
> "Do whatever He tells you."

Mary tells us the secret to life: "Do whatever He tells you." There are not many times we hear Mary quoted in the Gospels, so when she speaks, we must listen. At the marriage feast at Cana, Mary directs the servants to follow the instructions of her Son. Mary is also speaking to us when she says to "Do whatever He tells you" in order to be happy; "Do whatever

He tells you" to find God; "Do whatever He tells you" to find eternal life. The last recorded words of Mary offer us a clear path to salvation. Mary encourages us to follow Jesus at all cost. As Pope John Paul II said, "Our Lady does not presume to have any authority, even though she is the Queen of Heaven." Mary approaches us as a humble servant not only as His Mother but as His spiritual companion on His mission of salvation. As Mary brings her needs to Jesus, she also urges us to do the same. Bring your deepest cares to Jesus. Never hesitate to ask Him to intervene when things don't go as planned. Use Christ as your compass to guide your way. Listen to His voice and do whatever He tells you.

Mary invites us to be in communion with her Son. Through her pregnancy, Mary enters communion with Jesus. Mary points us to union with Jesus through our participation in the Eucharist and a life dedicated to Him. At the foot of the Cross, Mary lovingly consents to the sacrifice of her Son. She unites with Jesus in the Paschal Mystery. When we receive the Eucharist, we share in the Paschal Mystery as well.

Mary's presence after the Resurrection leads us to believe that she took part in some of the very first Eucharistic celebrations. Mary invites us "to imitate her relationship with this most holy mystery" (*Ecclesia de Eucharistia* 53a). Join Mary in her close relationship with Jesus. As the mother of our Savior, she held Him in her arms as a baby. She beseeches us to hold Him in our hearts. Our devotion to Mary will bring us to a greater understanding of her Son. The best way to Jesus is through Mary.

Life requires contemplation. From the moment of the Annunciation forward, Mary must ponder the possibilities of the future. Her incredible faith shows her trust in God. Her full surrender to God would not be possible without a life dedicated to prayer. When she and Joseph brought Jesus to the Temple, they encountered Simeon. He told Mary that "a sword would pierce her heart." Mary must contemplate the sufferings that would accompany the plan of salvation.

In the information age, we have become accustomed to accessing knowledge on demand. We pick up our cell phones or use "Google" to find out what we need to know. Mary showed that there is no substitute for prayer and contemplation. Mary was content to wait for God's plan to unfold. Mary wants us to incorporate the virtues of faith, hope and love. Faith pushes us to give ourselves completely to the Lord. Our mantra becomes "Your will be done." Hope anticipates the great things to come in this life and the next. No matter how difficult life may be, hope points to the possibilities of the future. Love brings all things together. It helps us to triumph over the sadness and misery of life.

Emulating the life of Mary helps us to eliminate the nonsense from our lives. Mary centers her existence on God and allows Him to work wonders in her world. Stop relying on having all the information before you act. Free yourself from the unnecessary fears of this world. Hand yourself over to the unknown. God has a plan for each one of us. Let His plan blossom as you weave faith, hope and love into your relationships. The woman from Nazareth holds the secrets for happy living. Join Mary in the humility of the stable. Stand beside her at the foot of the Cross. Implore the assistance of her Son as she did at Cana. Do not hesitate to ask our Mother to intercede on your behalf. When things seem chaotic and confused, pray. Let Mary's peace and consolation change your crazy life.

ENJOYING THE SILENCE

"We need to find God, and He cannot be found in noise and restlessness. God is the friend of silence. See how nature – trees, flowers, grass – grows in silence; see the stars, the moon and the sun, how they move in silence… We need silence to be able to touch souls."
Mother Teresa

One of my favorite extra-curricular activities has been moderating senior retreats. As we move into the overnight mode, I change roles. Sometimes Jesus requires us to wear different hats: teacher by day, watchman by night. Loaded with papers to grade, I sit in the hallway between the ladies and the young men while they sleep. "Why do you stay in the hallway all night?", they ask. "For a few reasons," I respond, "to make sure that everyone is safe and because I was your age once too!" I explain to my young friends that we do not condone "honeymooning" on retreat. Thankfully, they understood my role as chastity officer and they usually tuck into their own rooms without much protest. Once they are in their rooms, however, their lack of comfort with silence becomes apparent. The paper-thin walls of the old convent turned retreat house start to buzz. The students use their cell phones to call and text message each other. Their lights remain on and you can hear their iPods even with the earphones plugged in. The activity of these students on retreat is indicative of the frantic pace of our culture. We go through our days blasting our car radios, televisions, and personal listening devices as an accompaniment to the craziness in our lives. We continue to fill our world with noise because many of us fear what we may hear in the silence.

> Without taking the time to think about life, we are simply going through the motions.

We try to compensate for the existential vacuum by filling our lives with senseless noise. People today work and play harder than ever. When the chaos finally subsides, we find that our lives lack meaning. Psychologist Viktor Frankl called this "Sunday neurosis." Silence makes us contemplate our lives. In Frankl's time, Sunday was still a day of rest. Today it has become like every other day. We must find time for silence. As Socrates said, "The unreflected life is not worth living." Without taking the time to think about life, we are simply going through the motions. Before He began His ministry, Jesus headed to the wilderness to reflect on the journey ahead. The solitude of the desert helped Him to focus on His mission. Silence has tremendous benefits.

Silence helps us to learn about ourselves. We find out who we are in the peace and quiet. It gives us a chance to examine our lives. Tune out the noise and figure out the direction of your life. Many times we fill our days with emptiness to cover the realities that we don't want to face. In the silence, we can peel away the layers that hide our real selves from the world. The nakedness of the quiet exposes our vulnerability. We cannot be afraid to hear our true voice.

> Shut off the noise and pray with all your heart and put yourself in His presence.

Silence brings us to God. Psalm 46 urges us to "be still and confess that He is God." God knows that we tend to fill our lives with nonsense. When the noise of the day quiets, we can hear His voice. The clutter of our worldly concerns distracts us from recognizing His presence. He stands besides us, but we fail to see Him. Silence gives us the ability to see God. As Mother Teresa tells us in the quote at the beginning of this chapter, we need silence to foster the growth of our faith. In the quiet, we can hear the story that grows within our souls. Shut off the noise and pray with all your heart and put yourself in His presence. Jesus would tell us to find a secluded place and pray.

You may have heard why we have two ears and only one mouth: we need to listen twice as much as we speak. Silence makes us better listeners. Open your ears and listen to what others have to say. They may serve as our personal prophets pointing us to God's will. Some of the deepest communication occurs in the silence. We fill the air with endless chatter because it makes us comfortable when we are with others. Stand back and let others tell their stories. Learn the art of listening.

The hassled and frenzied pace of our world requires us to find a place where we can think. Do you retreat to a place where you can clear your mind? Some people find sanctuary at the beach. The gentle lapping of the waves remains the only sound for miles. We have a difficult time separating ourselves from our cell phones. It has become a practice in many parishes to ask the congregation to "silence" their phones during Mass. Inevitably, someone's phone rings during the Mass. Our desire for communication keeps us tuned in; however, our conversations have little substance. We speak often, but seem to have little to say. My students are bewildered when they hear that I refuse to buy a cell phone. "What if someone needs you while you are teaching?" They wonder. They forget that we remain accessible to others even though we do not have a phone at our fingertips.

Discover yourself in the quiet.

Monastic communities have used silence as a means of creating a prayerful atmosphere and working environment. Father Thomas Merton was a monk who understood the value of silence. He realized that the generalized noise of our culture assaults the inner self. It keeps us from "being truly present" in our lives. Merton said:

> Our service of God and of the Church does not consist only in talking and doing. It can consist in periods of silence, of listening, waiting. Perhaps it is very important in our era of violence and unrest, to discover meditation, quiet inner unitive prayer and creative Christian silence.

Merton urged us to explore our inner depths. He suggested the silent self within us must remain silent. To disturb it would be to destroy it. Silence for Merton was an opportunity to be with ourselves.

When Jesus faced the most restless moments in His life, He separated Himself from the crowds and withdrew into the silence. During His retreats, He found consolation and peace. We need to find our tranquility in the fruitfulness of silence. Discover yourself in the quiet. Shut off the television and the radio so you can hear the voice of God that calls you from within. Stop filling the air with senseless noise. Replace it with a profound prayer that grows from your heart. Meet the living God and the real you in the beauty of the quiet.

Becoming A Complete Christian
Part Two – Creating the Right Atmosphere

Read Luke 1:46-55 and reflect on the following questions:

1. How do I buy into the culture?
2. How does the culture build me up? How does it tear me down?
3. What are the possessions that are most important to me? Do they keep me from properly loving God and others?
4. How can I use Mary's example to find sanity in my life?
5. If you wrote your own Magnificat, what would it say?
6. What do I use to escape reality?
7. What changes can I make both internally and externally to create the right atmosphere?

PART THREE

OVERCOMING THE DAILY GRIND

THE WANT ADS

7

"A career is what you have; a vocation is what you are."
George Weigel

When I graduated from Chaminade High School in 1981, I thought I had the perfect career path carved out for myself. I had decided on a career in Law when I was 13 years old. As a senior at Chaminade, I participated in the collegiate program so I could shave a year off my time at Saint John's University. It seemed like the ultimate plan. So as I finished my time at Saint John's, I took the LSAT's so I could enter Saint John's Law School. But my scores on the Law School Admissions Test did not live up to my expectations or that of Saint John's Law School, so I had to make alternative plans. I planned to attend law school in the evening while I worked in Manhattan by day. I hoped that I could even find a company that would help me to pay for my additional schooling. With my resume in hand, I started the interview process. My cousin arranged an interview with his company in downtown New York City. At the interview, they hired me on the spot. Entry level positions were easy to find during this time. My responsibilities would be to act as a liaison between departments for this company. After paying for the commute into the city, there would only be a few dollars left to go out with my friends on the weekend. I contemplated the skimpy offer of my prospective employer on the train ride home. The prospect of working in the greatest city in the world was tempered by the meager wage and working as a glorified "paper pusher."

I arrived home by 2 p.m. and started my shift at the local deli at three. At work, I told Bill, the owner, my story. After I finished, Bill looked at me and said "As you know, we have been trying to sell the business. Why don't you buy the deli?" I never thought about owning my own business. Besides at 21 years old, where would I get the money? That night I laughed when I told my parents about Bill's preposterous proposal. But my parents didn't find it as ridiculous as I did. The next day they sat me down and offered to take a second mortgage on the house. I was floored by their act of faith. Within a few days, I had gone from going to law school, to working in the city, to owning my own business. I spent twelve years as the owner of Alex's Deli. I enjoyed my tenure there. I made a lucrative living, especially for a person in their young twenties. I believed that God wanted me in that place. I was able to help many people. I considered my time at the delicatessen as part of my vocation. God called me to that place for a certain purpose. I often thought that most people enjoyed their work; to my surprise, many people do not.

There are too many people who are miserable in the career they have chosen. I have a neighbor who absolutely hates his job. He leaves before the sun rises only to get home well after it has set. He complains about the uncivil treatment he receives at work. As Sunday night comes, he dreads the dawn of another week. Like others in similar situations, he will not quit because of the years he has invested in the company. Being in his 50's, he would rather count the years to his retirement than take a chance at a different job that may not offer the same salary or job stability. Most of us will work more than forty years of our lives. We need to find our true calling. This may mean that we will have to forsake a larger paycheck. Some people are lucky enough to find both. We should try to follow some rules in finding the perfect career:

> A job should be an extension of who we are.

A career should not be like a light switch that we turn on every day when we arrive at work and turn off each time we leave. A job should be an extension of who we are. Many people separate their work from the rest of their life. Our job can help define who we are. A career must be attached to our passions. Discover a job that you truly enjoy. It becomes easier to pour our hearts into our work when it is part of us. Work at a place that brings added joy into your life.

Our job should be like a prayer, something we offer to God each day as we sit in the office, the classroom, the factory or the store. Work with a purpose. Find a job with meaning. It should be part of our journey. A job should be a component of that which makes us fully human. It is important to approach our work as Jesus spent each day in the carpenter's shop in Nazareth. Even the most unpleasant task takes on meaning when incorporated with love. When work is considered a task of holiness, it transcends boredom and drudgery.

Choose a career that you are able to balance with your personal life. After playing in an Irish band for many years, I have found that the most successful restaurant owners are the ones who spend the most time at their place of business. You can't be married to your business and your spouse. Something has to give. I finally sold my deli because I immediately realized that I had some important choices to make. Life is too short to lose precious days with those you love. When your job begins to overtake other aspects of your life, it may be time to make some difficult decisions. Find a career that provides the opportunity to spend time with your family.

> Make your career something that fulfills you.

Some people take a job simply to pay the bills. Go with your strength. A job should highlight your talents and utilize your gifts. The biggest mistake that people make is taking a job that hides their ability. Don't forsake your passion for a paycheck. As Frederick Buechner stated, "The place where your deep gladness and world's deep hunger meet," is your true vocation.

If you are in a situation where you can intern for a summer or take a job on a trial basis, take advantage of the opportunity. Take a test run. We often concentrate on a subject area in college without ever seeing if we like that particular career. An internship gives a person a real feel for a place of work. If a job is not going the way you want, it may be time to move on. Don't get stuck in a job that leaves you empty. Time flies when you enjoy your work. Find a career where the days feel like minutes.

Choose a career that does not compromise your integrity. There are many jobs that allow us to make a living at the cost of others. The challenge to the Christian is putting off the material concerns of the world and focusing on Christ and others.

Evaluate the integrity of your job. Does your employer treat you and others with dignity? Make your job a place where you can practice kindness and charity.

Make your career something that fulfills you. When the alarm clock rings each day we need to look forward to the new day as an exciting adventure. Growing up does not have to mean that we can't have fun each day. The most prosperous and productive companies are run by people who are passionate about what they do. Look forward to each day you walk through the doors of your employment. Many people dread the sound of the alarm, while others cannot wait to awake for another chapter to unfold. The premise of Christianity is that everything is of consequence. The sacrifice of the cross makes us accountable for every moment that we live. Make every day count. Don't waste it in a job that leaves you empty. Let your work show the world who you are. Put meaning and fulfillment before salary. Let each paycheck be a surprise rather than a requirement. Live to work rather than work to live!

UP, UP AND AWAY

"The world is a book, and those who do not travel read only a page."
St. Augustine

My wife Allison and I love to travel. On our honeymoon, we traveled to the Caribbean. Soon after, we found ourselves venturing to Ireland and Italy. We fell in love with Europe. After our son Alex was born, we planned another trip to Italy during Holy Week and Easter of 1998. As many people do, we decided to make a quick stopover in England to save some money on our airfare. We had never traveled with a child before, but we certainly felt that we could handle it. At the time of the trip, Alex was 7 months old, so we figured he would adapt well to traveling.

Our trip from JFK Airport to London's Heathrow went off without incident. We left and arrived on schedule. But when we arrived at Heathrow, our stroller remained on the plane. Allison and I decided not to make a big fuss. "We will only be in London for an hour, so I can easily carry him around the airport," I rationalized. I didn't know at the time that our connecting flight would be delayed for five hours. Juggling a baby and your carry-on luggage can be a challenge, but somehow we survived and after a fifteen hour journey, we arrived in Rome.

Once settled into our hotel, we took a nap to compensate for our jet lag. Later when we awoke, Alex continued to sleep even as we toured the city. That night as we turned in for the night, Alex stood in his crib looking for playmates. We were exhausted, but because he caught up on his sleep during the day, we were now on opposite sleeping schedules. We laid Alex down and Allison and I drifted off to sleep. Suddenly, we awoke to the screams of "stuck, stuck!" Alex had tried to climb out of his crib but became entangled in the netting of the child's torture device that the Romans called a playpen. I realized that I had to tire out Alex if we were to get any rest at all. So at 2 a.m. I took Alex for a stroll. Our hotel was located only a quarter mile from the Vatican, so we walked towards St. Peter's. As I crossed the Ponte St. Angelo the frustration that I had been experiencing dissipated. Throughout the previous day, I had thought, "How can we survive in a foreign country with this little person?" I soaked in the beauty of an illuminated St. Peter's Basilica. It was then I realized that I must follow one of the major rules of traveling: when things are out of your control, you have to make the best of things.

The serenity of the Roman night made me appreciate my life, my family and my faith. The next day we attended Holy Thursday Mass with Pope John Paul II. Because of Alex's restlessness, we arrived a half an hour before Mass began. The only seats remaining were in the rear of St. Peter's Basilica. We had accepted the fact that we would only be able to see the Pope from afar. During the recessional, some priests and nuns saw that we were holding Alex and they motioned for us to come toward them. As we approached, they pushed us up to the railing hoping John Paul would see the baby and come to bless him. Their hope was fulfilled and our expectations soared when the Pope came over to us and blessed him and the rest of us who were next to him. What had started off as a nightmare had become the trip of a lifetime. Our willingness to travel with a baby made for a magical experience. Traveling has incredible benefits. It should become a vital part of every human experience. These are some of the important things to remember when we consider planning our vacations and why we should travel.

Travel opens our eyes to the world.

Travel allows us to experience new things. We become very comfortable in our own world and in our social circles. Many people I know plan their vacations to the same place, during the same week year after year. These vacations become reunions with families, friends and fellow vacationers. It is always great to work on these relationships; however, we want to challenge ourselves to experience new places occasionally. Move out of the ordinary. Don't be afraid to choose a place where you don't know the language or you are not familiar with the culture. Immersing yourself into a foreign atmosphere becomes an educational experience. It broadens your horizons. Traveling introduces us to new people. Talk to the natives to find out the real stories of a particular place. They will give you a true picture of a place while dispelling the myths and stereotypes of a culture that others misunderstand. The local people also reveal the best restaurants to experience the cuisine. Traveling opens our eyes to the world. For every place we visit, our world grows.

Create new memories with each vacation. I am always amazed when I hear my kids reminisce about past trips. They often speak about their fond memories of a particular beach, museum or restaurant. They can recall who they were with and what they had for dinner. These memories last a lifetime. The remembrance of a past vacation or the anticipation of your next trip helps us to overcome the days when the mundane consumes us. We bring our cameras and digital camcorders with us on our vacations, but the vacations we take leave an imprint on us that can't be replaced by photos or videos.

Traveling bonds people together. When you travel with people, you truly get to know them. I have vacationed with complete strangers and after only a few days, it seemed as if I knew them a lifetime. On vacation, you see how people react especially when the conditions are not the best. You may hear your children ask, "Are we there yet?" before you even pull out of the driveway. Be patient with your fellow travelers. Renew your relationships on vacation. Get away from the ordinary routine and spend time together. Experiencing new things together will create a bond that nothing can break.

> Experiencing new things together will create a bond
> that nothing can break.

Vacations break up the monotony of everyday living. The first thing the weary traveler says as they open the door and drop their bags is, "It's good to be home." Absence makes the heart grow fonder. We learn to appreciate what we have when we separate ourselves from them for a while. A vacation breaks up the ordinary routine. Sometimes the best cure for overcoming the doldrums is a call to the travel agent or booking a trip online.

Stop by your local bookstore and scan the travel section. Browse the travel web sites on the internet. Pick a destination and start planning your next vacation. Move out of your comfort zone and expand your possibilities. The vast world is calling you to adventure. Spend precious time with loved ones that will create memories that will last forever. Walk in the footsteps of Jesus in Jerusalem. Gaze upon the artwork of Raphael and da Vinci. Stand at the place where the first settlers stood when they landed on American shores. Enjoy the music of a reggae band while your feet are buried in the sand. Renew old relationships while creating new ones. Taste the food that reminds you of eating at grandma's on a Sunday afternoon.

Traveling will change the way you see the world and others. As Mark Twain said:

Travel is fatal to prejudice, bigotry, and narrow-mindedness, and many of our people need it sorely on these accounts. Broad, wholesome, charitable views of men and things cannot be acquired by vegetating in one little corner of the earth all one's lifetime.

See the world and open your mind to new possibilities. Drop into the small country church or the giant basilica. Discover how people of every age praise their God.

Meet the average person on the street and see what you share in common even though you live on opposite ends of the world. I have spoken with teachers from Africa who deal with the same difficulties with their students as I do even though major cultural differences separate us. The world is vast, but very little separates its inhabitants. Vacation is a "gift of God," says Benedict XVI, "that allows one to revive the physical and spiritual energies necessary for life's journey." Plan time to re-charge your batteries. Experience the world that God has put before you. Spread your wings and fly.

SHIFTING 9 GEARS

"When life gives you lemons, you make lemonade.
I have several stands around here."

James Brady

When people ask me about my most embarrassing moments in life, one particular situation comes to mind. Even though it took place nearly twenty years ago, it still seems as if it occurred yesterday. I stood behind the counter at the deli on a busy Saturday morning waiting on a customer. Sue was expecting her first child and was about five months into her pregnancy. Another woman noticed Sue and moved from the back of the line to engage her in conversation. "You look terrific, how much longer until the baby arrives?" she asked enthusiastically. Sue's eyes started to well up with tears. "I lost the baby last week due to a miscarriage," she said sadly. Suddenly the entire deli went silent. I finished Sue's order and she left without a word. Awkward scenes like this occurred often in a place where there was frequent interaction with others. One day I joked with a customer who rarely wore anything but dungarees or shorts, "Who made you get dressed in a nice suit like that?" He snapped back, "My father died and today is the funeral." Open mouth, insert foot.

Life throws us many curves along the journey. One moment we are on top of the world, the next someone pulls the rug out from underneath us. We have all witnessed someone we know who bought an extra car or a vacation home, only to lose a job because of company cutbacks. I recently pondered how to address some friends who had their first child. When the news of the birth spread through town, so too did the news that the child was born with Down Syndrome. "God blessed them with a beautiful baby," I thought to myself, but I realized that these young parents would have to adapt to the special needs of this child. This would require a lifelong commitment.

Often, my wife and I ask each other, "Do you want the good news or the bad news first?" Sometimes that's the way life goes: good and bad things happen at the same time. We may find ourselves asking, as Mother Teresa did, just how much adversity we will face:

> I know God will not give me anything I can't handle.
> I just wish He didn't trust me so much!

When we are faced with adversity, there are things to remember to help us keep our sanity:

Often, things are not as bad as they seem.

Adversity is unavoidable, so have "Plan B" ready. Assume that you will have bumps in life so when things go well, you can be thankful for the easier road. Be flexible. The more that we are able to adapt to our situations, the easier it will be to troubleshoot. We appreciate the sunny days more after an extended period of rain. Put things into perspective. Often, things are not as bad as they seem. Take the opportunity to count your blessings.

Adversity helps us to learn about ourselves. The challenges of life make us look deep inside and find the strength and courage we never knew we had. There are countless stories of people surviving in frigid conditions, with little or no food or water. Adversity makes humans transcend themselves. Their usual abilities and tolerances become extraordinary. As Pope John Paul II said about suffering in his Apostolic Letter *Salvifici Doloris*:

> It is one of those points in which man is in a sense "destined" to go beyond himself, and he is called to this in a mysterious way.

Embracing our adversity helps us to share in the suffering of Jesus on the Cross. We find our redemption by way of His Cross. There can be no Easter without Good Friday!

The difficulties of life bring people together. Through the gift of compassion, we share in each other's suffering. Compassion transforms sadness into joy through the gift of love. The greatest triumphs in life occur when we band together in solidarity. Don't go through life's difficulties alone. Allow people to help you. Look for a hand to pull you out of the hole. In turn, be a consoler to those who need comfort. We emerge from our own grief by helping others.

There can be no Easter without Good Friday!

Rely on your faith in God in times of difficulty. Suffering can shake the faith of the most steadfast believer. Cling to God in your times of difficulty. Talk to Him. Seek His guidance. By placing ourselves in His presence, we discover the love of God that takes on our suffering. Suffering may be unavoidable; however, He never wants us to face our struggles alone. We will join God in His Kingdom through this suffering. The glory of the Resurrection shows us that wondrous things can come from moments of humiliation and hopelessness. As Saint Paul said, "For as we share abundantly in Christ's suffering, so through Christ we share abundantly in comfort too." (2 Corinthians 1:5) It is through intimacy with the Father that we rediscover the "soul" which seems lost through our suffering (*Salvifici Doloris* 23). The only way to truly find ourselves is to give ourselves away. Hand yourself over to God and others in your desolation and grief.

There are times when we can put an end to our own misery. As Ralph Waldo Emerson explained, "Most of the shadows of life are caused by standing in one's own sunshine." Take a close look at your own difficulties. Don't sweat the small stuff! The way we deal with our problems will define what we have become. For some, the larger problems do not come from our adversity, but rather how we react to them. God pushes us out of the complacency of the nest to see if we are able to fly on our own.

Unite yourself with Christ in your times of difficulty. Ask Him for the gifts of determination, patience and courage. As the cold harsh winds of adversity fiercely blow, use the wind to your advantage and take flight. Learn from your trials. Find meaning in your suffering. Remember that after the long winter months of gloom, the flowers will bloom.

Accompany Jesus on the road to Calvary and He will help you to carry your cross. He will not leave you alone to suffer. He will dry your tears and wrap His arms around you. Rely on God to make sense out of the chaos. Find comfort in Him and the people around you. Share your compassion with others. The darkest night will lead to the most beautiful sunrise. Let that darkness lead to the light of Christ.

Becoming A Complete Christian
Part Three – Overcoming the Daily Grind

Read Luke 5:1-11 and reflect on the following questions:

1. Does my job fulfill me? Do I look forward going to work each day?
2. Does my job utilize my talents?
3. Does my job stand in the way of my relationships?
4. When did I take my last vacation?
5. What is my dream vacation? What is keeping me from taking it?
6. What are the things in my life that are keeping me from finding happiness?
7. What can I change immediately with a change in attitude?

Part Four
THE ESSENTIALS

LIVING THE CODE

"If God would have wanted us to live in a permissive society He would have given us Ten Suggestions and not Ten Commandments."

Zig Ziglar

When people think about the Old Testament, the Jewish leader, Moses, comes to mind. When Moses was called, he tried to rationalize his way out of it. "I cannot speak," came forth from his lips. God enlisted Moses' brother Aaron to be his speaker. The Israelites needed physical and spiritual leadership. They were a morally confused people. Like people of every age, their selfishness led them into trouble. When God summoned Moses to the top of Mount Sinai, He formally introduced Himself as Yahweh. God also wanted the Israelites to have some guidelines to follow. If they truly wanted to be God's people, they would have to be faithful to Him and His Law. The Israelites were swayed by the cultures that surrounded them. Even though the Lord led them out of captivity, the people believed in the god that suited their needs. They didn't consider their relationship with Him when they selfishly acted. They lived according to their subjective will. Relativism has been a problem of the ages. Pope Benedict XVI has been warning people about relativism for years:

We are building a dictatorship of relativism that does not recognize anything as definitive and whose ultimate goal consists solely of one's own ego and desire.

> Make God a priority in your life.

Moses also dealt with the "me first" generation. A moral code existed long before Moses came down from Sinai with the tablets. People simply chose to ignore the code. The Decalogue was God's wake-up call to a selfish world. In grade school, we memorized the Commandments as part of class. Most of us know them by heart. For the Christian, we are challenged to incorporate the old law and new law that Jesus gave us into modern living.

I. I am the Lord your God, you shall have no other gods but me.

Our faith in God does not only start the Ten Commandments, it begins all things. It is through His love, we are created. The ultimate sign of His love comes in the sacrifice of His Son on the Cross. Our lives must revolve around Him. The greatest obstacle of this relationship is falling prey to the distractions of the material world. Make God a priority in your life. Push away the distractions that keep you from loving Him as you truly can. Avoid worshiping the false idols that society presents as its gods. Don't allow the skeptics to make you lose your faith. Adore God as He deserves to be: with your heart, mind and soul.

II. You shall not use the Lord's name in vain.

The name of God should be revered at all times. In our culture, we invoke His name in anger and when we act in surprise to different events or circumstances. Because God desires intimacy with us, we should not reduce His name to a mere fact. The Israelites showed their respect for the name of Yahweh by writing it YHWH. Today the Jewish people would spell His name "G-D."

In the Our Father, Jesus reminds us of the importance of His "hallowed name." We must not take God's name for granted. By using His name in an offensive manner, we denigrate our Creator. By saving the use of God's name for prayer and promoting His glory we show our utmost respect for Him. Praise God at all times and remember the holiness of His name.

III. Keep holy the Sabbath.

The world we live in never sleeps. The Blue Laws closed stores on Sunday and made it easier to focus on God. Over the past twenty years, they have all been rescinded. The treadmill we are on never stops spinning. Sunday has become just another day. Incorporate God into your busy schedule. If you make attending Mass part of your routine, you will want to include it every week. Mass attendance brings families together. It makes marriages better. It provides a sanctuary in the midst of a chaotic week. Receive the Eucharist at every opportunity. Allow Christ to work miracles in your life. The Sabbath gives us the chance to physically put ourselves before Him and to show our appreciation for everything He does for us.

Make Sunday a time to focus on your relationships. Spend

time with God and the people in your life you love the most. Renew the glory of Easter each Sunday. Resurrect your faith and renew your relationships every week. Let the celebration that begins on the Sabbath carry on through every day.

IV. Honor your father and mother.

Today the importance of family has been forgotten. Fast food meals have replaced the family feasts. The pace of life had made us forego sitting together and engaging in true communication. The fourth commandment reminds us to foster family bonds. The strength of society relies on the stability of family life. Our families must be an extension of God. As the Catechism tells us, "When a family becomes a school of virtue and a community of love, it is an image of the loving communion of the Father, Son and Holy Spirit."

Although it may be a challenge, we must assist our parents even when raising children of our own. We are called to reciprocate the love they gave to us as infants. We may not agree with everything our parents say and do; however, we owe them our respect at all times. As God desires us to hear Him, He also wants us to listen to the ones who love us the most. Open your hearts and minds to your parents. Embrace the wisdom that they have earned through years of experience.

As parents, it is our responsibility to bring our children to Jesus Christ. We should allow them to meet God through the Sacraments. We need to incorporate a relationship with God into the life of our family. "The silence of Nazareth can teach the meaning of family life and the harmony of love" (Pope Paul VI).

V. You shall not kill.

This commandment calls for us to herald the sanctity of life. We should protect the unborn and make people aware of the devastation of abortion. When counseling those faced with an unwanted pregnancy, urge them to choose life. Supporting someone in this situation may cause us to be inconvenienced. An unwanted pregnancy can put a life into turmoil. The only remedy to this is love. Reach out to the elderly and provide comfort to those who are dealing with the difficulties of sickness. Touch others with the compassion of Jesus.

Most of us are not capable of cold blooded murder; however, we may not be aware that our words can kill another spiritually. Choose your words carefully and the effect that they have on others. Look around you and like Jesus did, bring the "spiritually dead" back to life.

VI. You shall not commit adultery.

This commandment recognizes the sacredness of our sexuality. Society promotes lust as an ordinary component of human nature. As Christians, we counter this philosophy with love and respect for the opposite sex. When we practice chastity, we honor God's gift of sex. Jesus lived as a model of chastity. He shows us that self-discipline and proper use of our freedom leads to communion with God and others through our sexuality.

Shield yourself and your family from the images and depictions of sexuality that demean us as humans.

A solid marriage is built on trust and fidelity. The marriage covenant is sealed through our bond in Jesus and should not be broken. The relationship between a man and woman reaches new heights when they are able to overcome the difficulties that exist because of personal faults and failures.

VII. You shall not steal.

Our respect for the property of others is at the heart of this commandment. Money makes us do desperate things. Fair wages should be paid for an honest day's work. Honor your business contracts. Don't take what does not belong to you. Sometimes we are under the impression that if we do not "take it," someone else will. Pirating movies, music and software is one of the major problems of today. Every time we make an illegal copy of something, money is taken out of someone's pocket. Fight the sin of greed. Learn the importance of moderation. Don't buy into the 'all or nothing world' in which we live. Too many people believe that the more we have, the happier that we will be. They are willing to do anything to gather as many possessions as possible. Seek heavenly treasures instead.

VIII. Do not bear false witness against your neighbor.

This commandment relies on the truth. Take responsibility for your words and actions. Inner peace is found when the truth is told. Stop gossip in its tracks. When we refuse to listen, others will have a smaller audience for which to spread their poison. When we unearth harmful truths about others, it is best to keep these things to ourselves. Sometimes people assume that we have completed a task when it is actually the work of someone else. Give people credit when it is due to them. Be the bearer of truth in all of your relationships. When the people in your life ask for your opinion, be gentle in your criticism. Assist others in correcting their faults. We must always remember to praise others for a job well done.

IX. Do not covet your neighbor's wife.

As an extension of the sixth commandment, we should practice the virtue of purity. A life of modesty helps us to live more closely to God. We must resist the temptations of unhealthy curiosity. In a world that encourages us to go after every urge and desire, we need to remember the importance of vows and covenants. A wandering eye means that you need to focus more on your own relationships. Satan knows our weakness for lust. Countering with love overcomes lust every time.

X. Do not covet your neighbor's goods.

The first step to happiness begins with our ability to detach ourselves from material possessions. The grass is always greener from the other side of the fence. Another person's material goods seem more impressive from afar. We assume that they will insure our happiness, but our possession of these things will guarantee nothing. Be content with what you have. Live more simply and practice generosity of heart. Recognize envy when it arises. Be appreciative of what you have and make the best out of what God has given you.

> The Commandments offer a practical, common sense look at morality.

When we live the Ten Commandments according to Christ's edict "Love one another, as I have loved you," we approach God and others in a new way. When love is incorporated into every commandment, we place the needs of God and others above ourselves. Our happiness relies on our fundamental attitude to live as Jesus preached and lived. The Commandments offer a practical, common sense look at morality. As God needed to remind the Israelites, we too need the direct guidance of His "code." God wants us to understand that every action is of consequence. Change this world through your moral example. Overcome sin with His generosity, poverty of spirit, temperance and gentleness. Grow as a Christian by cultivating God's goodness within you. Live the Code!

BLESSED ARE THE MERCIFUL

> "The quality of mercy is not strained; It droppeth as the gentle
> rain from heaven upon the place beneath. It is twice blessed.
> It blesseth him that gives, and him that takes."
>
> *William Shakespeare*

The Little Sisters of the Poor operate a beautiful nursing facility in Middle Village, New York. They care for many elderly women and men in a loving, peaceful and spiritual environment. The residents of Queen of Peace speak about how much they love their home provided by the Little Sisters. Every February, Queen of Peace hosts the Junior-Senior prom. Students from Kellenberg Memorial and Chaminade High Schools attend the prom and act as "dates" to the residents. My band, "The Irish Mist," provides the music for the evening. As the evening unfolds, I watch the students from the stage as they dance with the residents. Some of the residents can walk on their own power, but many rely on the assistance of wheelchairs and walkers. No matter what the health situation may be, the students and their dates dance the night away. I admire the courage and generosity of the students. Dancing does not come naturally to every teenager, never mind the student asked to dance with someone who is wheelchair-bound. The goal of our apostolic activities at Kellenberg and Chaminade is to connect the lesson in religion class to Christian living. In the Letter of James, he insists that as Christians, we must be willing to act on our faith:

> What good is it, my brothers, if someone says he has faith but does not have works? Can that faith save him? If a brother or sister has nothing to wear and has no food for the day, and one of you says to them, "Go in peace, keep warm and eat well," but you do not give them the necessities of the body, what good is it? So also faith of itself, if it does not have works, is dead. (James 2:14-17)

The Christian life remains empty without mercy.

Jesus knew the emptiness of words. Too many people talk a good game, but when it comes to doing, they come up short. Jesus cured on the Sabbath because He wanted to show us that formal worship is not complete without loving action. Throughout His entire ministry, Jesus exhibited the necessity of helping others. Jesus urged His followers to reach out to others in their time of need. St. Thomas Aquinas defined mercy as "a heart suffering over the suffering of others." Thomas formalized what the Church calls the Corporal and Spiritual Works of Mercy. The Christian life remains empty without mercy.

Corporal Works of Mercy

1. *Feed the hungry.* Share what you have with others. So often we take our abundance and luxury for granted. Poverty and hunger could be wiped away if we ended waste in society

and in our own lives. Take notice of what you put into the garbage each day and think about how you can assist others.

2. *Give drink to the thirsty.* We must spread joy and hope with those who are empty and alone. So many people long for spiritual nourishment. They hunger and thirst for kindness and love. Become the well that quenches the thirst of those who search for consolation.

3. *Clothe the naked.* It is our obligation to protect the weak and exposed in our world. We should not rest peacefully in our warm homes if we neglect to notice those who are left shivering in the cold night. Extend Christ's warmth to others.

4. *Visit the imprisoned.* Jesus challenged His followers to care for even those who experienced difficulties in their lives. Help others find conversion through your presence and example. Loving the sinner while despising sin is perhaps one of the greatest obstacles to Christians.

5. *Shelter the homeless.* We should reach out to the unloved and unpopular in any way we can. Homelessness does not only refer to those left out on the streets. There are many people estranged from their families and loved ones. Help reconnect those who have become separated because of family arguments and rifts.

6. *Visit the sick.* Be there for those people in your life with health issues. Help those who are isolated because of disease and sickness. Your visits can banish the silence of loneliness and provide evidence of a caring community. A cheerful presence can change the mood of the sick and put them on the path to recovery. Just knowing that people care can be the medicine they need.

7. *Bury the dead.* No one should grieve alone. Most people dread attending wakes and funerals, but the more people who

take on the suffering of others, the easier it will be for those to overcome grief. Have compassion and be a good listener to those who have suffered. Provide comfort with kindness and prayers.

Spiritual Works of Mercy

1. *Admonish the sinner.* Challenge the things that you know are wrong. Point others to God through your example. We should resist the sin of omission as we fail to act when others do wrong in our presence.

2. *Instruct the ignorant.* Everyone takes on the role of teacher at different points in their life. Instill your wisdom in others. Tutor others on the secrets of life and show them that true happiness can be found in a relationship with God. Share your advice gently.

3. *Counsel the doubtful.* The world is filled with many who are uncertain about what to do. Our suggestions may fall on deaf ears. When we show that we care, people are more apt to listen. Speak honestly and from the heart.

4. *Comfort the sorrowful.* Be a shoulder to lean on in times of sadness and hurt. Look even for the smallest sorrow and disappointment as opportunities to share hope and optimism. Every person who takes on the sorrow of others decreases it by bearing its weight for others.

5. *Forgive all injuries.* Bear wrongs patiently. By forgiving others who do wrong, we practice the mercy of Christ. Mercy allows us to heal and places the sinner on the road to God. Deal kindly with those who do thoughtless things and help them to correct their ways.

6. ***Pray for the living and the dead.*** This simple act can become a great challenge especially as our lives become busier. Make prayer an integral part of every day. Spend time remembering others in your life. Prayer connects us with God and others. This will become the simplest way to help other people in our lives.

> Look to the needs of others before you act.

Embrace a more compassionate way of life. Look to the needs of others before you act. Each day presents tremendous chances to the good of Christ in the world. As the *Catechism of the Catholic Church* states, "the works of mercy are charitable actions by which we come to the aid of our neighbor in his spiritual and bodily necessities." Many people around us need our help. Our Christian life is not complete without extending our hands and hearts to others as Jesus did. We should practice mercy with everyone we meet. Make the Beatitude "blessed are the merciful for they shall receive mercy," a central theme in your life.

Becoming A Complete Christian
Part Four – The Essentials

Read Matthew 5:3-10 and reflect on the following questions:

1. Which Beatitude best describes me?

2. Which commandments do I struggle with the most?

3. Do I find myself committing the same sin over and over? What can I do to change these actions?

4. When was the last time I went to the Sacrament of Reconciliation?
5. Which "works of mercy" do I practice in my own life?
6. How can I be more compassionate to others?

PART FIVE
SCULPTING THE SOUL

MR. AND MRS. POPULARITY

"Popularity is the easiest thing in the
world to gain and it is the hardest thing to hold."

Will Rogers

Our family's dinner ritual is similar to most others. At one point
in the meal someone asks the question, "How was your day?"
One night my son, Alex described his day. He told about the
exploits of one of his classmates. Alex explained that "Joseph"
was one of the "cool" kids. My wife and I looked at each other
in disbelief. Even in kindergarten, children were branded as
popular or unpopular. Popularity has become something that
we notice from the youngest age. Even if we do not say it aloud,
everyone wants to be recognized for who they are. When we
walk into a party we hope that others say, "I'm glad you came!"
Selfishly, we may desire popularity, but in the end it may be
selfishness that keeps us from being popular. When we allow
selfishness to grow, we build a wall that keeps others from
ourselves. The generosity of Christ attracts others to us. There
are simple ways to discover this spirit:

Recently I heard a story of a widow who was going through
her husband's belongings after he had passed away. When she
found the Medal of Honor that he had been awarded during
World War II, the children were awestruck that their father

had received such a tremendous honor. "Why didn't you tell us about this before?" the son asked his mother. "I never knew," she responded. While the children pondered why their father had kept this secret to himself, the mother said calmly, "We didn't need to see the medal to know he was a hero!" The mother revealed the truth about heroes – real heroes never boast. Bishop Fulton Sheen described humility in his book, *Thinking Life Through*:

> Saints never speak of their holiness; that is why it is difficult to portray a truly religious man on stage... The real saint keeps his virtues hidden, but the man who would impress others with his holiness must cultivate a certain tone of voice and even join his fingers in an attitude suggestive of prayerfulness.

We have all encountered the overly dogmatic person who tries to compensate for a lack of knowledge. As Father Powell said in *Why Am I Afraid To Tell You Who I Am?*, exaggerated behavior is the opposite of what it implies. We try to cover our insecurity by overcompensating. The truly humble person lives a life of service to others. Humility places others before ourselves. The process of elevating others quietly raises us at the same time.

> Be interested rather than trying to be interesting.

Be interested rather than trying to be interesting. Be present to others. Selfishness makes us worry only about ourselves. People appreciate when you take an interest in their lives. Learn about others by listening to their stories. Push aside the distractions that keep you from engaging others. Recognize how the other person feels. Connect with them emotionally. Set aside the prejudices that keep you from hearing the truth. Walk in another's shoes to understand what they are experiencing. When you spend time talking only about yourself, the spotlight only shines on us. Don't leave others in the dark. Focus on the need for others to be heard.

The more you show your true self, the more others will appreciate you. Be sincere. Stop playing the games that keep you from being authentic. We become afraid of acting as ourselves because of the fear of rejection. When we put forth a false persona, people do not fully accept us, because it is not who we truly are. Show others your inner goodness and recognize the goodness in others. Recognize the talents and strengths of others. Avoid criticizing and ridiculing others. According to Fulton Sheen, "Ridicule covers up the disgust of one's own life by projecting that disgust on others." Build others up with confidence through your positive words. People fear the gossip because they never know what the gossipers will say once they leave the room. The popular person has enough self-esteem that he doesn't have to tear others down to build himself up.

Staying positive is a key to drawing people to us. Everyone remembers the classic *Winnie the Pooh* books by A.A. Milne. Winnie the Pooh has two friends who show the extreme attitudes in life. Tigger demonstrates the qualities of the total extrovert. Tigger maniacally bounces everywhere he goes. His unrestrained enthusiasm makes everyone smile. He heads into every adventure without much thought. Eeyore stands at the other end of the spectrum. He always expects the worst in life to happen to him. Fun and spontaneity have no part in his life. Each day for Eeyore offers no new possibilities. These two characters illustrate the different approaches that we can take towards life.

Everyone loves the person who sees the best in life. I am not speaking of the person clouded with delusion. The realist, who seeks the best in everyone and everything, brings out the finer qualities of those around him. The devil's advocate has his place; however, the person who believes that a plan can succeed usually finds a way to execute it. As Winston Churchill said, "A pessimist sees the difficulty in every opportunity; an optimist sees the opportunity in every difficulty." If you want the admiration of others, make things happen. Look at the brighter side of life and incorporate that which Jesus brought into a despairing world.

Loving others will make you more lovable.

In our search for popularity, we should look at some of the principles Jesus gave us. The more we seek popularity, the less we will encounter it. When Jesus spoke the words, "The last shall be first and the first shall be last," He knew mankind's inclination for self-promotion. He understood our desire for power. The greatest avenue to power is popularity. We hold elections to determine who holds the most power. Every November, we hold these glorified popularity contests. The more we put others in front of ourselves, the more others will respect us. Stop worrying about how others feel about you. When you love others with all your heart, your popularity will grow. Loving others will make you more lovable. Not everyone we encounter will love us or even like us. Be yourself and people will love you for who you are. When we allow others to take precedence over ourselves, our reward will not only be popularity, but a place in heaven.

REAPING WHAT YOU SOW

"Pray as though everything depended on God.
Work as though everything depended on you."

St. Augustine

Shortly before Allison and I were married, we purchased our home. We could only afford a "handyman special." We found a treasure that needed a tremendous amount of work. The house was owned by an older woman who now resided in a nursing home. The previous winter, Dorothy had fallen causing her to need around the clock assistance. With the house being vacant, no one realized that the oil tank was empty. The weather in New York during the winter of 1994 was brutal. The above normal snowfall and record low temperatures caused havoc on this old house. When the pipes froze, they exploded causing the dining room ceiling to collapse and the oak floor to buckle. When I showed Allison the house for the first time, I feared that the damage in this room would intimidate her from buying it. My father eased her anxiety and reassured her that all of the damage could be repaired. When the pipes cracked, the water flowed down the walls. The surface coat of plaster on the walls remained wet almost a year later. My father advised me to remove this layer of plaster. "Scraping the layer off the wall would take weeks!" I thought. When I questioned my father looking for an easier solution, he explained that sometimes in life the only recourse is patience, diligence and hard work. So as I set out to restore the dining room, I heeded my father's advice and scraped a few feet of the wall each day. Within a week, the task was completed.

In the hours I spent working on this project, I contemplated another important lesson I learned a few days before I began my tenure as an owner of a delicatessen. Standing in the walk-in refrigerator, I sought an elusive, lone pickle in the murky brine of a pickle bucket. I tried to avoid immersing my hand and arm because of the chilly temperature of the liquid, so I searched for the rascal with a pair of tongs. The current owner of the deli witnessed my futile poking and chastised me. As he sternly said, "If you don't put the effort into this business, you won't last a year," I started to contemplate my work ethic. I knew that success would elude me if I did not put in real effort. This pivotal moment in my life echoes in my mind daily.

These two stories remind us of the old adage, "You reap what you sow." What you put into this life, you will get out of it. We live in an age where people offer short cuts and quick solutions to some of life's bigger challenges. Those who have gathered wisdom with age would warn us that there is no substitution for hard work.

Radical changes do not happen overnight.

Sometimes, we have to take small steps in order to get things done. The expression, "Rome wasn't built in a day," reminds us that beautiful things take time and dedication to evolve. Practice patience in everything you build, especially your relationships. Radical changes do not happen overnight. As we grow, we take baby steps before we are able to run. When we look back on our relationships, we can see how they have grown with time. True knowledge of each other happens over the course of a lifetime. Our society worships immediate gratification. The answers seem to always be one click away. Real solutions demand time and forbearance.

Everything must be accomplished with the same love and effort. I constantly question my students on their careless attitude towards school and homework. As they fall into the pit of senioritis, I ask them how they think they will fare next year in college with this attitude. They rationalize that things will be much different because of their desire to be in college. When we look at our list of tasks to be completed, we often choose the jobs we like to do rather than the ones we dislike. We must approach each task the same way. Helen Keller reminded us of this when she said,

> I long to accomplish great and noble tasks, but it is my chief duty to accomplish humble tasks as though they were great and noble. The world is moved along, not only by the mighty shoves of its heroes, but also by the aggregate of the tiny pushes of each honest worker.

The bigger tasks will seem more impressive when the smaller jobs are completed with great love.

When we work hard, we reap tremendous rewards.

Many of us dream of striking it rich one day by hitting the lottery. We push away reality through the delusion we create. As Thomas Jefferson declared, "I'm a great believer in luck and I find the harder I work, the more I have of it." We can create our own good luck through diligence and perseverance. The more effort, the better the results. Very few people have found success without sweat and blood. When we work hard, we reap tremendous rewards.

As a person involved in pastoral counseling, I deal with people looking for solutions to their problems. As parents, we have to tend to the needs of our children; as spouses we must make our marriages a priority; as students we will not succeed without putting effort into studies. We must find the balance to taking care of ourselves and others. There are no easy solutions. We have all encountered a co-worker or fellow student who tried to skate through life using their charm and great personality. A smile, a good joke and a firm handshake can only take us so far. Don't hesitate to reinforce this with dedication and effort.

Good deeds will always be rewarded. New age religions refer to this as "karma" or in other words, "what comes around goes around." In the busy world, people overlook acts of kindness and generosity. We may say, "Why bother?" when our efforts fall into the existential vacuum. Jesus calls us into service to assist others, especially the least of our brothers and sisters. Enter into a life of humility and love. You will experience the incredible feeling of self-satisfaction. Our reward awaits us in the next life even if it is ignored in this one.

Many people may not realize that the theme from this chapter came from the Bible. Saint Paul gave practical advice in his Letter to the Church in Galatia. He wanted these early Christians to understand that salvation is found through Jesus

Christ and His sacrifice on the Cross. Performing good deeds will unite a person with the crucified Christ.

> For a person will reap only what he sows, because the one who sows for his flesh will reap corruption from the flesh, but the one who sows for the spirit will reap eternal life from the spirit. (Galatians 6:7-8)

Faith and action must be integrated into a life with Christ. Saint Paul's exhortation to Christian living must become second nature to us. Jesus lived the motto: anything worth doing is worth doing well. No act should be done in vain. Everything for Him was performed with love. Put the effort into life and you will not be disappointed. Treat each day as if it's your last and love each person as if it's Jesus, Himself. Plant the seeds of Christ's love every day. They may not grow immediately, but the harvest will bear abundant fruit.

LAYING THE FOUNDATION

"Faith is taking the first step even
when you don't see the whole staircase."
Martin Luther King, Jr.

With the exception of haggling with the salesman, buying a new car can be a thrilling experience. As you stroll through the showroom, you envision yourself in each car. The cars radiate on the showroom floor. It becomes difficult choosing the car of your dreams. Finally, the day arrives to pick up your car. When you open the door and slide behind the wheel, the distinct new car aroma hits your nose. Everyone loves that smell. The salesman sitting in the passenger seat gives you an orientation tour of the car. You can't believe that this car is yours! The salesman hands you the keys and you insert them to start the car. With the keys in the ignition, you turn them, but nothing happens. You look at the salesman in disbelief. "What's wrong?" you ask. "Oh, if you wanted a car with an engine, that's extra!" he insists. You get out of the car to look for yourself. When you open the hood, you confirm the salesman's words. It's empty as you feared. As you stand back to examine the car, you realize why you chose it, it's absolutely beautiful. But without an engine, the car is no more than a shiny hunk of metal.

I used this exaggerated story to convey the predicament

of humanity. We care so deeply about our external appearance that we often forget to worry about what dwells inside us. Many people look great on the outside only to be empty within. We focus on the superficial and overlook the status of our spiritual lives. Without God, our existence is incomplete. Many people feel that they can live apart from God and be happy. They replace God with useless alternatives. They delude themselves into thinking that they can be fulfilled without Him. I pose my theory to my students every year. Predictably, there is always the one student in the class who insists that they know an atheist who has found happiness, even in a life separated from God. "If I didn't believe in God or heaven, I would be miserable," I interject. We exist as beautiful, but empty shells without God.

Saint Paul wrote in his Letter to the Romans:

> Therefore, since we have been justified by faith, we have peace with God through our Lord Jesus Christ, through whom we have gained access (by faith) to this grace in which we stand, and we boast in hope of the glory of God. Not only that, but we even boast of our afflictions, knowing that affliction produces endurance, and endurance, proven character, and proven character, hope, and hope does not disappoint because the love of God has been poured out into our hearts through the Holy Spirit that has been given to us. (Romans 5:1-5)

We pile on the excuses of why we tend to leave God out of our lives. Most people simply replace God with more tangible alternatives. They are not consumed with grudges or resentment towards Him. It comes down to the old adage: out of sight, out of mind. We deal with the mundane rather than the heavenly. But in the process, we neglect an important piece of the puzzle. Without it, we are not whole. Recently, I attended Mass with a friend. At Communion, I motioned that he take the place ahead of me in line. He said that he was not in the state of grace to receive the Eucharist. He had not attended Mass in years. He lives a good moral life, but unfortunately, puts God at the bottom of his list of priorities. After Mass, I urged him to jumpstart his relationship with God. He needed to go to Confession and start fresh. He insisted that he didn't need organized religion to lead him to God. He believed that he and his family were doing well in their present spiritual state. My friend is among the majority of Christians who have fallen away from active practice. I hear the stories everyday. "I just don't go anymore," they say. We slowly slip away from God into oblivion. Consumed by selfishness, our relationship with God suffers. When people ask me how to reestablish their relationship with God, I answer:

We must use prayer as the cornerstone to building a better relationship. As in all of our relationships, communication is imperative. Prayer paves our way to God. John Paul II said that "prayer is the first verification that man is a religious being, capable of putting himself in contact with God." For this Pope and many saints, prayer sits at the heart of our search for God. Open up your world to God through small conversations each day. Speak to Him in moments of desolation and include Him in your times of joy.

> Awaken the thirst for God that lies deep in your heart.

Enter the world of "Eucharistic amazement." The Pope insisted that the Eucharist is the soul of all Christian living.

The Body and Blood of Christ is a heavenly treasure that we can experience here on earth. Through the Eucharist, we share in the Paschal Mystery. Let Holy Communion transform your life. Bow before Him in Eucharistic Adoration. Allow the grace that flows in this sacrament to penetrate your being. Come to the banquet and feast. Discover the gift that Jesus wants you to receive. Become one with Him and share in His glory.

John Paul started his papacy with the words, "Do not be afraid" and "Open wide the doors for Christ." A relationship with Jesus Christ answers all of the challenges and difficulties of life. The Pope showed us that we can dispel uncertainty and find truth in Jesus Christ. Embrace the Cross of Jesus and bring consolation into your world. Pope John Paul II assured us that we should never be afraid to trust God or a life of faith. Surrender to the will of God. Awaken the thirst for God that lies deep in your heart. The Pope traveled the world to reveal "the secret" of Jesus Christ to the masses. To live attached to Jesus requires courage, but at the same time we can find our fulfillment in Him.

Open the doors of your life to Christ. Permit Jesus to lead you from the darkness to His light. Dependence on God is not a sign of weakness, rather an indication of wisdom. As humans, we place too much emphasis on "seeing to believe." Hand yourself over to the unknown. Stop allowing your eyes to determine what your heart desires to see. Turn to Jesus and center all things on Him. Make weekly worship an important part of your life. The time to strengthen your relationship with Christ is now. Create a life that will be a prelude to everlasting glory. Incorporating God will make all things better. Invite God into your life today.

GOD BESIDE ME

"Aim at heaven and you will get
earth thrown in. Aim at earth and you get neither."

C.S. Lewis

Author George Weigel has been called one of the most articulate intellectuals on the American theological scene. He was given the enormous task of writing the biography of Pope John Paul II. In his masterpiece *Witness to Hope*, Weigel rose to the occasion telling the incredible story of one of the 20th century's greatest figures. During the final days of John Paul II, the world listened to Weigel as he recounted stories on the life of the beloved Pope.

> The people we meet, the community where we live, the items we use, can all lead to God.

In his book, *Letters to a Young Catholic*, Weigel speaks about the importance of experiencing the world as the "arena" where God redeems us. A major part of our Catholic faith can be affirmed in the tangible realities of the world. We encounter God through the gift of our senses. Weigel reminds his readers of "the core Catholic conviction that God saves and sanctifies the world through the materials of the world." This is called the sacramental imagination. Many people who look at Catholicism from the outside, assume that it robs the faithful of the material treasures of the world. The opposite is true. Since Catholicism is sacramental, it relies on tangible items that point us to a deeper relationship with God. When used properly, material things can help us to experience the Divine. We need to find God in the ordinary and accessible. Saint Ignatius of Loyola urged us to sense God in all things. The people we meet, the community where we live, the items we use, can all lead to God. The worldliest things could potentially remind us of His divine presence. The sacramental imagination permits us to take a culture that is moving away from Christ and utilize it to invite Him into our lives. Our goal as Christians includes transforming the earthly into the heavenly:

Make mealtime a place to experience the Divine. As the Eucharist invites us to the table of the Lord, every meal can provide a chance to nourish ourselves spiritually. The fast food world prohibits families from spending quality time together. We have developed the "eat and run" mentality where there is little chance to engage others. Americans have used mealtime as a way to catch up on work by eating at a desk or bypassing the meal altogether. The less time we spend around the table together, the less time we have to enjoy the company of others. Don't wait for a holiday to set aside time for a meal together. Take the opportunity to catch up on your relationships every day while enjoying God's bounty. Many times we refer to a dining experience as "heavenly." A deliciously prepared meal can elevate the cook through sustaining the needs of others. Those invited to the feast may experience the transformation of an earthly treasure bestowed on us by God.

Jesus challenged us to recognize Him in every person we encounter. He urges us to use our relationships as an avenue to God. The sacramental imagination proposes that our relationships channel a deeper union with Christ. Every time we touch others physically and spiritually, we influence our connection with Jesus. When Jesus presents the requirements for entrance to heaven, He uses very concrete directions of feeding, clothing, visiting and caring for one another.

In his teaching on human sexuality, John Paul II said marital sexuality becomes a sacrament that reveals as much about God as it does ourselves. The human body points us to God. The sacredness of the human body should not be taken for granted. The Incarnation highlights the importance of this gift. God enclosed our souls in the perfect package. We must use this present to nurture our relationship with Him.

As Saint Teresa of Avila reminds us, our bodies take the place of Jesus on earth. We have become the earthly representatives of Christ. Faced with temptation, suffering and evil, we have been given the ability to transcend everything through our communion with Him.

Recognize God in the beauty of nature. Get outside and enjoy the best of the Lord's playground. Take a walk and soak in the glory of His world. Even in solitude, we feel the real presence of God when we experience nature. Anne Frank declared:

> The best remedy for those who are afraid, lonely or unhappy is to go outside. Somewhere they can be quiet, alone with the heavens, nature and God. Because only then does one feel that all is as it should be and that God wishes to see people happy, amidst the simple beauty of nature.

Nature instantly connects us with God. Through God's creation, we learn about the infinite nature of our Creator. The Creator's masterpiece draws us closer to Him. God paints the most stunning landscapes to make us aware of Him. The more we experience nature, the more certain we can be of His existence.

> Experiencing the sacraments brings us to Christ.

We should actively participate in the sacraments. They are the sign posts that point us to the direction of God. Experiencing the sacraments brings us to Him. Christians can become complacent in our approach to worship. We forget the jewel at every Mass is the Eucharist. We should make the reception of Christ our priority. This sacrament summarizes the Paschal Mystery which redeems humanity. The priestly mediator invites us into communion with the Father.

Resolve the things that keep you from a relationship with God. Jesus passed on the ability to forgive sins to the Church. God awaits every one of His children to return to Him. Reconcile your relationship with God, and make the sacraments an integral part of your faith life.

The major challenge for the Christian in the new millennium is recognizing evidence of God in a secular world. The sacramental imagination makes God accessible in ordinary living. Whether we find ourselves in Mass or in a social setting, we can meet the transcendent. Any person we encounter or any object we use opens up the possibility of experiencing God. Too many of us search for the miraculous epiphany, when we should look no further than the ordinary to discover God.

Open your eyes and see Him in the people you come across. Taste His goodness in the daily bread He provides. The immanence of the Almighty pervades things large and small. He plants reminders of His presence all around us.

The "Breastplate of Saint Patrick" summed up the sacramental imagination. Patrick supposedly wrote this beautiful prayer as he battled paganism:

> Christ be with me, Christ within me,
> Christ behind me, Christ before me,
> Christ beside me, Christ to win me,
> Christ to comfort me and restore me,
> Christ beneath me, Christ above me,
> Christ in quiet, Christ in danger,
> Christ in hearts of all that love me,
> Christ in mouth of friend and stranger.
> Find Christ in all things and all things
>   will lead you to Christ.

Patrick unveiled God's presence in the pagan world of the early Irish. He used their common symbols and gave them divine meaning. He knew how God worked in the world: He dwells in all things and awaits our discovery. Listen to Saint Patrick and make his prayer your own. There are many paths to Him, take any one.

Becoming A Complete Christian
Part Five – Sculpting the Soul

Read Mark 10:35-52 and reflect on the following questions:

1. Do I consider myself popular?
2. Why, or why not, am I popular?
3. Would others consider me a hard worker? If not, why?
4. Do I have an elevated sense of self-importance?
4. Into what things in my life do I need to put more effort?
5. Do others consider me selfish?
6. How do I overcome my selfish tendencies?
7. How do I tend to my spiritual life? How often do I pray? How often do I attend Mass?
8. How do I experience the Divine daily?
9. Do I recognize His presence every day?

PART SIX

FINDING GOLD IN YOUR RELATIONSHIPS

GREAT EXPECTATIONS, WHERE DID THEY GO?

"You learn to speak by speaking, to study by studying, to run by running, to work by working; and just so, you learn to love by loving. All those who think to learn in any other way deceive themselves."

St. Francis de Sales

Sunday afternoons at the delicatessen were the slowest time for business. During this time, Billy, a clerk at the store and I would stand at the front window and watch the world pass by. Often, we would see young parents taking a stroll with the father pushing the carriage. Since the father was probably the same age as me, we looked at this guy as if his life was over. "Look at this poor guy," we would cackle from inside the safety of the glass. "Surely, only death could give this man release from his sentence," we thought. It wasn't until I found myself pushing a stroller that I understood what the young father experienced. The maturity of fatherhood made me realize the beautiful and yet simple nature of love.

Love has been glamorized in the movies since they were invented in the beginning of the 20th century. A woman meets the man of her dreams and by the end of the movie, they ride off into the sunset. All is good with the world. When we see love portrayed, we are usually given a glimpse of ideal love.

We associate love with the tremendous rush of feelings. We contemplate love at a wedding or the birth of a baby. Each year I see parents beaming with pride at graduation. After the ceremony, they hug their children outside the arena. I hear the chorus of "I love you's" as I make my way through the crowd. Occasionally, I pass the student who spent countless hours in the dean's office and barely passed to graduate. I wonder, "How did this parent who gushes with pride today react to the scores of failing grades because their child refused to do any work the last four years?" Life challenges us to love each other especially when we are particularly "unlovable." Love is an act of the will. We choose to love. Real mature love requires effort. Jesus lived as a human being to show us how to love each other. Betrayal, failure, and ignorance were never reasons to stop loving. For Jesus, the misgivings of those people around Him made His love ever more present. From Bethlehem to Calvary, Jesus poured out His love on the world. Many times humanity didn't seem interested in returning that love. It did not stop Him from making the supreme sacrifice for us. True genuine love does not demand a response.

The romantic or erotic love portrayed in our culture gives us a false perception of love. We must resist the temptation of attaching ourselves to the glory of romantic love. If we love only when the stars are in alignment, our fantasy world would be shattered when reality hits. Robert Johnson referred to loving through the ordinary as "stirring the oatmeal" love. He stated:

> Stirring the oatmeal is a humble act – not exciting or thrilling. But it symbolizes a relatedness that brings our love down to earth.

> Love shines in the quietest moments of life.

Johnson compares the act of love to the act of stirring oatmeal. Most days, love is not very exciting. Many people sleepwalk through the week, only to come to life on Friday as they leave work or school. The rest of the week means nothing more than taking care of the mundane aspects of life. We cannot save love for a special occasion. We must, as Johnson reminds us, "find meaning in the simple, unromantic tasks." As we care for an elderly relative, change the baby's diapers, take out the garbage or pay the bills, we must remember that everything done with love takes on new meaning. Love aspires to do what the ego does not find fulfilling. Love conquers the smallest tasks. Love shines in the quietest moments of life. It allows us to transcend the ordinary. As Saint Paul tells us, "It bears all things, believes all things, hopes all things, and endures all things" (1 Corinthians 13:7). When a spouse has an accident with the family car, when another report card comes home with unsatisfactory grades, or when a parent lets us down, we must delve deep into the well of love to make things right again. Love will overcome every circumstance. As the daily problems of life assert themselves, loving others brings Christ's peace into our lives.

The love of Jesus is different because it pushes the boundaries of ordinary relationships. It radically demands that we alter the way we approach every person that we may encounter. Love becomes a light that illuminates a selfish world. It ignites the heart that has grown cold with skepticism and doubt. Love puts no limits on itself. It is as infinite as Christ Himself.

As parents, children, spouses, colleagues and friends, we

must constantly challenge ourselves to think of others first. The love of Jesus must motivate us to become other-centered. Love takes practice or as Erich Fromm said, it must become an "art." Love must be included into every realm of our living. Without love, we are like birds without wings. We can never reach our true capacity as humans without love. Practice love every day. There are simple ways to make love a reality in your life.

Make an effort to do something positive for someone each day. Perform random acts of kindness. A kind word of encouragement or a simple gesture can change another's path in an instant. It only takes a moment to stop and recognize the needs of others. When you ask someone, "How are you?" stop and listen to their story. Ring the bell of a neighbor that you haven't seen in a while and say "hello." Be the initiator of good in the world around you. The results will be magical.

> Make an effort to do something positive for someone each day.

Since love is an act of the will, we must choose to love. True mature love does not stand on the sidelines. Love will not bloom with us attached to the couch. Move into action. Laziness and apathy are the enemies of love. Respond to the needs of others. Overcoming selfishness will bring us into communion with others. Each day we have the opportunity to assist others. No act is too small when it comes to love.

Practice making love part of you. Learning to love is similar to mastering an instrument. The more we work on the craft of loving, the better we will be at loving. Love must be part of the fountain that flows from deep within us. The more we love all of the people in our lives the better we will be able to blend the relational chords of life.

There will be days when you may not "like" particular people in your life. Love must be unconditional. Love never takes a holiday. We should love even when people disappoint us. No matter what the circumstances may be, love always wins. Jesus lived this love on the Cross on Good Friday.

Open your Bible and read the greatest love story ever written. From Eden to the empty tomb, we encounter God's endless love for us. Jesus shows us that love begins and ends with our willingness to help others. Look to Jesus and discover true love. Follow Him to the Cross and experience the deep connection that He shares with each of us. Love will live up to your expectations, if you love everyone the same. It cannot let you down, if you live up to your end of the bargain. Open your heart and love. Practice until it is perfect.

THE DATING GAME

"Dating should be less about matching
outward circumstances than meeting your inner necessity."

Unknown

At the end of senior year, we discuss love and marriage as part of our curriculum. Ultimately, one student asks me where I met my wife. I pose this question to them. Do you think we met: a) at a church, b) through a friend, c) online, d) in a bar? I am always curious to hear their responses. Because I teach religion, most students assume that my life revolves around church. "You picked her up at one of those parish dances," one joker recently blurted from the back of the classroom. Usually after a five minute discussion and once all of the laughter has subsided, I reveal to the students that I met my wife at a bar. I had met many girls that I dated in bars. My friends and I always frequented places that featured great bands. I love music and I have played in a band since college. Our nights in Manhattan usually ended at Fleming's Pub on the upper east side of New York. One night it all was different and my life changed forever. As the clock neared midnight, a young woman passed me who I thought was absolutely beautiful and without thinking I told her so. I have been with Allison ever since.

Dating allows us to meet people. Even as an important step before marriage, some people take this stage of life for granted. Sometimes it's less about relationships and more about sexual recreation. Dating has evolved through the years and it is interesting to see how young people approach this process. My students explain the steps of dating as:

1. *Talking to him or her.* Two people test the "waters." They establish a comfort zone between each other. They text one another and write to each other via the computer. This becomes a period of getting to know a person before there is any discussion of going out together.

2. *Hooking up.* This is a purely physical stage of the relationship. The two people are not exclusively in a relationship at this point. During this part of the relationship a person decides whether they are sufficiently attracted to the person.

3. *Being together.* The couple does various activities with each other as they enter an exclusive relationship. Although "together," this stage allows each of the partners to exit the relationship when they feel it is time to move on.

4. *Dating (Going Out).* Both people have committed to the relationship. They have reached an "official" exclusiveness in this stage. The world now knows that they are a couple.

> Failure to take risks in our relationships can paralyze us.

The dating ritual of young people today demonstrates their fear of getting hurt. We ease into our relationships because we worry about rejection. Failure to take risks in our relationships can paralyze us. We have all seen the "trust game" where one person falls backwards into the arms of another. We can never be totally sure that the person behind us will catch us before we fall, just as we may be uncertain of the status of a dating relationship. Why does a person seem "head over heels" in love one minute and then move on to another relationship? We need to differentiate between infatuation and true love. "Head over heels" is pure infatuation – blindness at its best. Columnist Ann Landers wrote an inspiring article about the difference between love and infatuation.

Infatuation is instant desire. It is one set of glands calling to another. Love is friendship that has caught fire. It takes root and grows – one day at a time. Infatuation is marked by a feeling of insecurity. You are excited and eager but not genuinely happy. There are nagging doubts, unanswered questions, little bits and pieces about your beloved that you would just as soon not examine too closely. It might spoil the dream. Love is quiet and understanding and the mature acceptance of imperfection. It is real. It gives you strength and grows beyond you – to bolster your beloved. You are warmed by his/her presence, even when he/she is away. Miles do not separate you. You want him/her nearer. But near or far, you know he/she is yours and you can wait.

Dating can be treacherous at times. We may enter into a relationship where the other person's expectations completely contrast our own. We can feel as confident as walking on solid ground or experience the uncertainty of sinking into quicksand. We can never totally predict actions and desires of another. Some people hide their true selves for fear of not being liked for who they are, so they play games instead.

Many Christian writers have offered their advice on dating. Hopefully, these ideas will serve as practical guidelines to the person dating in the new millennium.

Choose venues where you can learn about each other. When I dated, I avoided activities such as going to the movies or attending concerts on dates until I had a chance to get to know the person. Look each other in the eyes and see if you have things in common. Learn whether or not you share the same passions and goals. Working on communication from the first date starts the relationship off on the right foot.

> Treat her like a queen and him like the man of your dreams, even if this is not the person that you may marry.

There is an old saying, "A new broom sweeps clean." We tend to be at our best when a relationship is new. Show the true lady or gentleman you can be. It becomes a challenge to maintain these standards. When you incorporate respect into the relationship, you can keep the relationship at its optimum level. Treat her like a queen and him like the man of your dreams, even if this is not the person that you may marry. Remember the dignity of the person during every encounter. Relational chivalry never goes out of style.

Too many people feel that they can't do any better than the person they are with. Never settle! We must become comfortable being alone, especially when it may be better to be alone than being in a relationship that brings us down. Put yourself out there and date as many people as you can. Don't be closed minded and reject someone simply because bells do not ring when they walk into the room. Choosing the person you will marry is one of the most important decisions you will ever make. Enjoy the social aspects of dating and meeting people. Every date does not necessarily have to lead directly to marriage. Learn the qualities that you desire in your future husband or wife.

> People will respect you for making a commitment to purity.

As we date, we become dependent on the physical aspects of our relationships. Lust lures us away from true love. When I love the other person, I consider what is best for both of us. Lust leaves us empty and robs us from the true communion that awaits us in the sanctity of marriage. Contemplate your boundaries and limits before you find yourself in the passion of an embrace. Speak about the goal of abstinence in your relationships. People will not fall in love with you more quickly because of your willingness to have sex. He or she will respect you for making a commitment to purity. Leave room for the Holy Spirit to work magic in your relationship.

Incorporate God into your relationships. If you are a spiritual person, make no excuses for a life devoted to God. If you feel spiritually disconnected, look to Christ for relational answers. Attend church together and make God a priority. Spend time in prayer together. Elevate each other through a relationship with God. A happy marriage uses the bond of Jesus to solidify it.

Dating must be more than an audition for marriage. The person you choose to marry must be a true friend. Make sure that he or she recognizes your talents and goals and supports them. Don't overlook differences that can cause a rift in your relationship. Dating helps to discern whether or not philosophical and existential differences exist between two people. Love conquers all, but there may be things that may be too difficult to overcome. Ask yourself the important question, "Can I love this person forever?"

Enjoy this social stage of your life. Bringing God and love together in this process will lead you to a fruitful marriage. Bring the truthfulness of Jesus into dating. Eliminate the game playing and be authentic. Showing our true selves to others can be scary. Have confidence that the person you date will accept you as you are. Put love at the center of this relationship and let Christ take over.

I DO, FOREVER

18

"Marriage is the mother of the world. It preserves kingdoms,
and fills cities and churches, and heaven itself."

Jeremy Taylor

During World War II, Viktor Frankl was imprisoned at the
Auschwitz concentration camp. Frankl was separated from his
wife when they entered the camp. As he worked many grueling hours, the thought of his wife brought him consolation.
On occasion, Viktor would gaze at the sky as the stars faded
and the sun rose. He imagined himself speaking with her. His
wife seemed to shine even more luminous than the sun. As
Frankl contemplated his marital relationship in *Man's Search
For Meaning*:

> A thought transfixed me: for the first time in my life
> I saw the truth as it is set into song by so many poets,
> proclaimed as the final wisdom by so many thinkers.
> The truth – that love is the ultimate and the highest
> goal to which man can aspire. Then I grasped the
> meaning of the greatest secret that human poetry
> and human thought and belief have to impart: The
> salvation of man is through love and in love. I under-

stood how a man who has nothing left in this world may still know bliss, be it only for a moment, in the contemplation of his beloved.

I often share this meditation with my classes when we discuss marriage. Especially from a male standpoint, marriage gets a bad rap. When men speak of marriage among themselves, you hear derogatory terms such as "prison," "monotonous," and "restrictive." I once attended a bachelor party where the groom's friends chained a bowling ball to the ankle of the groom for the evening. We describe marriage as something that ties us down. People portray it as an inhibitor of freedom. When I announced my engagement, women seemed thrilled to hear the news while the men offered their condolences. Too many of us forget the reason why we decided to get married. Years have erased the anticipation and excitement as we waited for our wedding day to arrive. Time has blurred the magic of our courtship. Our vows have become just the words that people say at their nuptials. They have lost their meaning. I often ask my students to look around the restaurant next time they go out to dinner and look at the couples. They notice that many of these couples go through their entire meal barely uttering a word to each other. Recently, I saw a man nudge his wife to the other side of the table so he could secure a clear view of the basketball game that he wanted to watch. His eyes never wandered from the television and they ate dinner in silence. Marriage for some has become a death sentence.

Christian marriage binds us to Jesus. He becomes a partner on our journey together. This relationship should enhance our marriage. Jesus works as our greatest counselor in times of difficulty. Following His guidance we can have a successful marriage. When I notice a couple who have a successful marriage I ask them their secrets. Here are some jewels of wisdom that have been passed on to me:

Remember the earliest days of your relationship. Rekindle that magic and keep the romance alive. Think about the qualities of your spouse that drew you to him or her initially. Romance will remain in a marriage if you put the effort into it. Our careers, children and other preoccupations can distract us from focusing on our spouse. Remember to keep this relationship as a priority. Spend quality time with each other. Schedule a date where the two of your can look into each other's eyes and rediscover the beauty of your relationship. Cherish the quiet moments together. Steal away for an hour or two. Take a stroll together and hold hands. Plan activities that you both enjoy.

When your spouse has a difficult moment, lighten his/her mood. Make each other laugh and find humor in the chaos and difficulty in life. Another role of the spouse is to make the other person better and to elevate each other. My wife often reminds me when I am being unreasonable. She provides an objective perspective when I am unable to see the truth. Spouses should bring one another into communion with God and others. Remind one another when you enter the shell of selfishness. Jesus pulled His disciples back into the circle of responsibility. We need to act as He did in His friendships. Being a better person will make your spouse a better person. Those around us feed off of our moral leadership. My wife tells people that she is riding my coat tails into heaven, when actually it is her kindness and understanding that makes me a better person. Lead each other to heaven. In union with Christ, we can find eternal glory together.

> Spouses should bring one another into communion
> with God and others.

It is vital that spouses support each other. Take an interest in his/her job. Learn about the responsibilities of their work and what his or her job entails. Meet your spouse's colleagues. It is much easier to relate to a tale from work, if you can put a face to a name. Ask about her day with the kids. What may seem mundane to you might be the highlight of your spouse's day. Listen with an attentive ear. There is nothing more frustrating than when we feel that others don't pay attention to us as we pour out our hearts.

There are ultimately things that our spouse finds fascinating that we do not. Support his/her passion and allow them to express themselves. People need an outlet that provides release from the daily pressures. Whether it may be on the softball field, through art, stopping for a drink with friends, or even time alone, we must give our spouse their own personal time to unwind.

Respect is a vital component of love. This allows us to see the differences that exist between us, yet still appreciate each other. Respect also keeps us mindful of the dignity of the other person. In every situation, we need to take into account the feelings of others. When dinner doesn't turn out to be the meal we were looking forward to, we should tell the cook how much we appreciate their effort. When the freshly painted room looks completely different than we pictured, we should praise the work of our spouse who spent endless hours painting. Respect for our spouse requires us to think twice before speaking. My wife always reminds me, "It's not what you say, but how you say it." I have spent many nights at dinner with couples who seem to despise each other. Their words cut each other. They fail to realize that they have lost all respect for each other. When respect is gone, a relationship quickly deteriorates. Work on respect in your marriage and you will see your spouse in a different light.

Welcome children into this world. Children can bring a marriage to new heights. Children magnify the love of the couple. As Fulton Sheen said, "Love by its very nature, wants to bear some fruit." Children are the fruit of that profound love. The love that the couple gives a child returns tenfold to the parents. Children turn us from our selfish ways. They make us realize how we need to refocus ourselves to others. God wraps His most precious gifts in the children He gives us. Share in the role of creation and love and bring children into this world.

Marriages based on a relationship with God stand a better chance of enduring than those that exclude God. Build your marriage on a solid foundation. Invite Jesus into your marriage. A relationship with God takes effort. Family life has become busier than ever. Our weekends fill up quickly. Put God on the schedule. If you don't plan for it, it may not happen. Make weekly attendance at Mass a priority. "The family that prays together, stays together." Place visible signs of your faith inside and outside of your house. Be proud of your relationship with God. Remember that inviting God into your marriage will strengthen it. Immerse your marriage into Christ and discover the commitment He shows for His Church. Serve one another in His profound love. Extend the love that you share with your children and illuminate your family with His light. Bring the salvation of Jesus to your true love.

Remember that inviting God into your marriage
will strengthen it.

Married life is an incredible part of our lifelong journey. If you are lucky enough to find the right person, enter into this beautiful covenant. Live the adventure together. Hold each other through the sorrows and laugh at the craziness. Set goals and seek joy in every day. Celebrate your love as life unfolds before you. Live and love together, forever!

EVERYTHING'S RELATIVE

"Today we are faced with the preeminent fact that,
if civilization is to survive, we must cultivate the science of
human relationships… the ability of all peoples, of all kinds,
to live together, in the same world, at peace."

Franklin D. Roosevelt

Growing up in an Irish/Italian family, every holiday became a huge gathering. My mother was one of five daughters. Her brother died shortly after birth. I was blessed to be one of twenty-one cousins. We enjoyed great summers in Rockaway Beach, New York. People called Rockaway the "Irish Riviera." Families rented bungalows to escape the city heat in the summer. As you walked the boardwalk, you would have been able to find us by our beach umbrellas clustered in a group. A few rolls of eight millimeter silent film still exist. These movies capture the magic of those days. Time has sweetened the memories of my childhood, but there is no denying that this time in my life was special. My grandfather, a retired New York fireman, proudly presided over the festivities each day. When the *Angelus* bells rang each day at noon and 6 p.m., all activity ceased and everyone on the beach stood silently in respect. When the bells finally subsided, we resumed our games of running bases, swimming, sand castle construction or whatever activity we were doing.

There were certain cliques that existed in our group of cousins. The groups were divided by age. Six cousins belonged to our group. We were separated by no more than four years of age. We played endless hours together during the summer. We could go months without seeing each other and continue our conversations where we left off at our next gathering. These relationships made Thanksgiving, Christmas and Easter magical. We didn't care about dinner, only spending time together. After these holidays ended, we experienced a real letdown because of the absence of the company of the other cousins. When we see each other today, we reminisce about those wonderful days of our childhood.

Today, I enjoy watching my kids with their cousins. The echoes of laughter ring throughout the house each holiday or whenever they get together. They love spending time together. Each vacation rivals the next one. My wife and I have tried to teach our children that there is no substitute for the bonds that we create in life. Our relationships are the treasures from a life well lived. Some friendships evolve from nothing into truly beautiful things. There are key components to fruitful and fulfilling relationships. We should incorporate these components into all of our relationships.

> Our relationships are the treasures from a life well lived.

We must work at all of our relationships. Every relationship requires effort. We might have to pick up the phone to make a call to show our commitment to a relationship. Clear your calendar to make time for others. In the 24/7 world, we tend to overlook some people in our lives because of our hectic schedules. Make time for those you really care about. When others shut you out, help them to open their eyes to resolve the problems that exist between you. Seek out these people in your life who have fallen into the void.

The only way to know where you stand in many relationships is to communicate. Communication allows us to reveal our true selves to others. We need to articulate our feelings to one another. Talk about the obstacles that exist in your relationships. Learn what lies deep within each other by communicating. Don't let time distort your disagreements. Resolve conflicts as they arise. Simple fights can snowball into major feuds if you allow them to fester. We tend to dwell on our problems and blow things out of proportion. Life is too short to lose time because of these conflicts. Assume the role of the peacemaker. Bring others together before a rift separates them forever.

Be present to each other.

The pace of our society drives us to endlessly multitask. I constantly remind myself to resist the urge to check my e-mail or finish work on my computer when a student stops in my office to chat. Turn off the cell phone or the television and look someone in the eyes and really listen. Put your energy into one relationship, one moment at a time. Be present to each other.

Learn to forgive the people in your life when they wrong you. Forgiveness lifts the burdens that weigh us down and keep us from discovering true joy. Admit when you make a mistake and seek forgiveness for your missteps. The words "I'm sorry" can change everything.

Show a greater understanding for another's situation. Stop

working according to your own rhythm and examine the needs of others. Step back and see the big picture. The practice of counting to ten and allowing a moment to pass before reacting is a prudent one. Avoid falling victim to the pace of society that urges us to always hurry. Show patience.

As we spoke about the topic in an earlier chapter, love makes everything better. When love exists in a relationship, it soars to new heights. Love makes us ask ourselves the question, "What is best for the other person?"

Working on your relationships keeps them alive and vibrant. Look to Jesus and see how He related to those around Him. His best friends failed Him when He needed them most. Instead of terminating the relationship, He pushed it to a deeper level. Many families or friendships turn a blind eye to major problems that exist. Jesus did not ignore problematic situations. He called people on their infidelity, their greed, their envy or their lack of faith. Be honest in your relationships. Discover true joy in relating to those around you. Relationships help us to build the bridge between this life and the next. The accumulation of wealth and riches can never fulfill you like your relationships.

We must love in order to be loved.

Be aware of the differences that exist between you and others. Recognize the complementary qualities that make two people whole. Share time with others and create memories that last a lifetime. If you remember the story of the tax collector Zacchaeus, he climbed a tree to get a better look at Jesus. Like Zacchaeus, we must be willing to go out on a limb in our relationships. Don't allow your fear of getting hurt keep you from taking risks. We must love in order to be loved. Christ knew the risks, but He never hesitated to call people to Him. Like Jesus, some may misunderstand and reject us. However, these failures did not deter Him. Jesus showed us how to find gold in our relationships. Remember our relationships with those around us will have a bearing on our relationship with God and on their relationships with God.

We can become complacent in our own little world of isolation. Knock down the walls that keep you from loving others. Have real relationships with true communication. Emulate Jesus as He sat at the table and desired to know others more deeply. Sit, talk, listen, learn and love!

Becoming A Complete Christian
Part Six – Finding Gold in Our Relationships

Read Luke 10:8-42 and reflect on the following questions:

1. Do I recognize my relationships as the most important thing in my life?
2. Do people know the real me?
3. What keeps me from showing others my authentic self?
4. How can I filter out the distractions of this world and put myself at the feet of Jesus like Mary?
5. Do I treat others with the respect they deserve?
6. How can I be a better boyfriend/girlfriend, husband/wife, son/ daughter, father/mother and friend?

THE MISSING PIECE

Whether I enter a classroom or sit down to write I always have one main objective. I want my audience to understand that the secret to happiness can only be found in a relationship with God. There are others, especially in our society who would have you believe differently. Too many people walk through this world, without discovering the missing piece. We must never forget as Christians, that our greatest gift is Jesus Christ. Through Him, with Him, and in Him, we must do all things. He must become the central figure in our lives. For us to be complete Christians, we must integrate this relationship into everything we do. Those who read my books can tell that I teach by my inclusion of a review chapter at the end of every work. Here's a brief overview of the many points in *The Complete Christian*.

1. ***Being Christians requires us to live differently.*** People should look at us and know that we are Christians by the way we act, what we say and how we present ourselves in the world. When we are confused and do not know how to act, we need to look to Jesus as our example.

2. ***The Christian life revolves around conversion.*** Throughout our earthly existence, we must reevaluate our lives and determine how we need to change. Don't wait until Advent and Lent to think about your spiritual well-being. Emulate Jesus in

all that you do and make changes today.

3. *We must learn to love ourselves.* Without self-love, self-acceptance, and self-esteem, we can never truly love others and God. Recognize your talents and what you bring to this world. Be gentle on yourself and laugh at your mistakes. Look into the mirror in love to find who you are.

4. *The media and pop culture tend to leave God out of the equation.* Since the culture does not embrace God, we must include Him. As citizens of the 21st century, we must make sure that people are aware of His divine presence. Society has shown the more it excludes God, the emptier it becomes. Do not let a Christo-phobic world keep you from celebrating your God.

5. *Silence in our lives can lead to true peace.* Tune out the noise and listen to the voice of God. Shut off the distractions and truly speak to Him. Solitude and quiet will bring us into His presence. In the silence, you will discover the real you that is camouflaged by the distractions of the world.

6. *True devotion to Mary is devotion to Jesus Christ.* As a human, Mary lived a life of perfection and grace. Follow her example and you will walk beside Christ as she did. Live with Mary in your heart and find consolation in your most difficult moments and joy in every day that you live.

7. *A job must become more than a paycheck.* Find a job that fulfills you and becomes part of you. When the alarm clock rings, we should look forward to the day ahead. If each day you dread going to work, it is time to get a new job.

8. *The vacation is important for your spiritual and physical health.* Use vacation as a time to reacquaint yourself with the important people in your life. Expand your world and see new things and meet new people. Get out of your comfort zone and create new memories that will last forever.

9. ***We must be able to shift gears when things go wrong.*** Things may not always work out as we plan, so we must have alternatives. Learn from your suffering and make lemonade out of the lemons that are given you. Remember that we are united with Jesus in our suffering. Use adversity to look deep within yourself and reach new heights.

10. ***The 10 Commandments serve as our moral guide.*** In a world where relativism reigns, this code presents a clear guide to living. Know the Commandments and apply them to life. Show others the way to live by your moral example.

11. ***The Christian life should be one full of mercy.*** As Christ shed His love and compassion on the unfortunate, we too must practice mercy in our lives. There are many who suffer in our midst each day and we must be sensitive to their needs.

12. ***The true path to popularity is through humility.*** Spend time giving yourself to others and popularity will come naturally. The more we put others before ourselves, the more people will recognize our generosity and kindness. Remember: "the last shall be first."

13. ***The more we put into life, the more we will get out of it.*** People constantly search for shortcuts, but there is no substitute for hard work. Your relationships, your job, your faith life and every component of your being require time and dedication. Anything worth doing is worth doing well.

14. ***As Christians, we must become Eucharistic people.*** Active participation in worship is vital to the Christian life. A relationship with God requires a life of prayer and contemplation. Schedule time to be with Him every week. Permit Him to dwell in your life.

15. ***Since God created all things, we should be able to find Him in even the ordinary.*** Whether you are sitting at the beach,

enjoying a good steak, or hanging out with friends, use it as an opportunity to find God.

16. *Love should be incorporated into everything we do.* Without love, every action remains empty. Love can never happen if we remain stagnant. We must understand the importance of love in our lives and make it a reality. Use the Cross as the symbol of true love. Wrap your love around everyone you meet.

17. *Dating is an important part of the marriage process.* Dating should help us to find the person we want to spend the rest of our lives with. Date with dignity, respect, and chastity. Dating should be the beginning of a friendship that lasts forever.

18. *Marriage is a sacred covenant that takes a lifetime to fulfill.* Society has made marriage a disposable relationship. We must restore the sanctity and holiness to marriage through our love and commitment to each other. Remember the wonderful qualities of your spouse and what drew you to him or her initially.

19. *Our relationships are the most important things that we have in this lifetime.* Cherish these gifts. True relationships are the gold waiting to be discovered by you in this life. In order to find this treasure, you must be willing to work. Spend each day crafting something beautiful.

Embrace Jesus and help others to find Him. Find the path to eternal happiness in your relationship with God and others. Show others that you are His disciple by every action and word. Be proud of your connection with Him. Start the process of becoming a complete Christian today.

ST PAULS

This book was produced by ST PAULS/Alba House, the Society of St. Paul, an international religious congregation of priests and brothers dedicated to serving the Church through the communications media.

For information regarding this and associated ministries of the Pauline Family of Congregations, write to the Vocation Director, Society of St. Paul, 2187 Victory Blvd., Staten Island, New York 10314-6603. Phone (718) 982-5709; or E-mail: vocation@stpauls.us or check our internet site, www.vocationoffice.org